Men

FIRING THROUGH
ALL OF LIFE

AL STEWART

blue bottle
BOOKS

Men
Firing through all of life
A Blue Bottle Book
Published September 2007

Blue Bottle Books
PO Box A287
Sydney South NSW 1235
Australia

Ph: (612) 8268 3344
Email: sales@youthworks.net
W: www.publications.youthworks.net
National Library of Australia
ISBN 978 1 921137 86 0

Cover design and typesetting by Richard Knight Design
Cover image: 1959 Cadillac

To Kathy—the world's most patient wife.

The first half's been good.

The second half will be even better.

Introduction: One day in autumn
Section 1 Groundhog Day

Chapter 1 Midlife—the good news
Chapter 2 The midlife train arrives
Chapter 3 The conspiracy
Chapter 4 What hasn't happened
Chapter 5 The bricks in the wall
Chapter 6 Some more bricks
Chapter 7 Ancient wisdom

Section 2 The search for answers
Chapter 8 Pleasure, partying and possessions
Chapter 9 Money
Chapter 10 Sex, pornography and withdrawal
Chapter 11 A frustrated universe

Section 3 A radical solution
Chapter 12 Eternity in our hearts
Chapter 13 The punch line that changes everything
Chapter 14 The biggest life
Chapter 15 A revolution lived out
Chapter 16 Revolution 2—Service not selfishness
Chapter 17 Revolution 3—Faith in action
Chapter 18 The revolution on the ground
Chapter 19 Midlife (and beyond) worth living
Chapter 20 Surviving and thriving.

Conclusion

Appendix A
Men and midlife—Exercise and the physical

Appendix B
Middle-aged men and sex

I'd like to thank Simon Smart
for the hours he put in to help make
this book happen. Thanks mate
for your encouragement, feedback
and editorial skill.

Introduction

One day in autumn

One Saturday in April, while I was sitting at my desk, I had the following email exchange with a long-time friend:

'This urgent calling of nature longs to be tested, seeks to be challenged beyond itself. The warrior within us beseeches Mars, the god of War, to deliver us to that crucial battlefield that will redeem us into the terrifying immediacy of the moment. We want to face our Goliath so we may be reminded that the warrior David is alive, in us. We pray to the war gods to guide us to the walls of Jericho so we may dare the steadfastness and strength of our trumpet call. We aspire to be defeated in battles by powers so much greater than ourself, that the defeat itself may have made us larger than when we arrived. We long for the encounter that will ultimately empower us with dignity and honour. Be not mistaken: the longing is there and it's loving and terrible and beautiful and tragic.'

Richard Heckler, *In Search of the Warrior Spirit*.

Jack

I replied...

It's a perfect autumn day, bright blue sky, and I am sitting in my office on my day off, working, and there's three more things I'm supposed to prepare in the next two days as well.

Outside I've got a ridgeback, old and with arthritis who lies on a foam mattress waiting to die, although at least he doesn't know it. I sometimes feel that my life and his are similar, but then maybe I'm kidding myself. He was bred for hunting lions in Rhodesia, and a few times I saw him get the chance to do what he was bred for, well at least in miniature (with pigs) and man he could do it. And I realised those were the times he was really alive, but most of his life, 99% has just been being soft and lying on the mattress and being bored, or asleep, and now his back legs are going. What was I bred for? I just feel like it was more than sitting on the lounge, (inside the house, instead of outside like the Dog)—waiting to die—or getting arthritis so I can be a problem to my children.

I wonder if growing older is just the slow process of dreams dying, of realising that it will not happen as you dreamed, that you never will fight that giant; that you never will succeed in those things you've quietly dreamed of but never told anyone because you'd have been too embarrassed. You are not going to play cricket for Australia or write that bestselling novel. So many things that you could have done, maybe should have done, but now the cords of obligation slowly wrap around you (little by little as the people of Lillyput tied up Gulliver—cord by cord).

We wake up one morning and ask 'How did I get here?' but don't really want to face the question. We want to be better husbands and fathers than we are, and yet we slowly turn into our fathers. We want our kids to suck the marrow out of life and yet they make the same choices and mistakes that we made.

So we stay and love our kids and wives as best we can.

The warrior, the hunter, the explorer are fantasies. We just can't do these things, can we? Life may have been short for them, but they knew they were alive. We lie on the mattresses at the back door and feel comfortable, bored and half asleep or half alive, but comfortable. We worry about trivia and amuse ourselves with the TV like the rest of the huge sleepy herd, as our dreams die one by one. I see it now, but I didn't see it when I was 18, or 20. What could I have done? I want to say to my son, 'mate—life is so short, you can do anything, make sure you live, take risks, fight your giant, choose things that will make you afraid. At least then you will feel alive.' Suburbia emasculates us.

I think you may understand all this. I don't know if it is testosterone that makes for the turmoil, or what.

Now I'm not asking you to solve anything—don't think 'he's finally flipped'—don't counsel me, don't show anyone else this silly email, and don't worry about me. I'm just feeling annoyed and sorry for myself because I've been stuck in the city for four months without a break and I'm working on my day off. Just keep being a good mate, just by being there you're a life-line to sanity.

Will be good to see you on Monday,

Lester *(the nickname he uses for me)*

Jack replied...

That is exactly it Lester! You understand why I sent it. I understand what you wrote, and we continue on in faith, believing that somehow this slow, boring, death by a thousand geeks is actually the same as heroic faithfulness, and someday Jesus will say, 'well done mate, what you did was tougher than standing in the Coliseum, cause you just stood there in suburbia like I asked.' Or something like that... Doesn't require counselling or advice or sympathy, just endurance...But... 'Be not mistaken: the longing is there and it's loving and terrible and beautiful and tragic.'

Jack

I wrote...

Hey Jack—thanks for the reply.

You do understand! I reckon you might be the only one on the planet. I spoke with one of our guys who's a Major in the Army the other day, and he was talking about putting his name down for a special forces course. It would also mean maybe going to East Timor. I couldn't get my mind back on the job for about ten minutes, I was supposed to be giving him marriage counselling, but all I could think about was how fantastic it would be.

I appreciate having you around mate.

Anyway... enough existential angst for one day. I went for a run on dark tonight—5kms in 22:24, not great but it was good for the soul. The boy came with me on his bike, it was fun.

Lester

Henry David Thoreau (1817-62) wrote, 'The mass of men live lives of quiet desperation'. This touches a chord with many of us. If he was right 150 years ago in his assessment of how many of us live, it's surely even truer today. Why does this happen to us? Does it have to be this way? Are there any answers?

This is a book for men asking questions in midlife

The midlife crisis has become a cliché, but men do reach a point when they begin to ask questions. What is life all about? How did I get here? What do I do with the second half of my life? Where exactly did my 30s or 40s go? How come every day seems like 'Groundhog Day'? Is this all there is? Questions about marriage, and family, and jobs, and success and failure, and God, are ones that midlife has a tendency to throw up at us, sometimes unexpectedly.

Men may ask these questions with varying degrees of angst, but most of us will ask them at some point. Asking the questions is a good thing, but how about some answers? What do we do? Sometimes the wrong reactions to midlife have disastrous results, for our lives and the lives of others.

This is a book for men who want to fix something

Sharing worries and giving sympathy is nice, but men want to fix things. This book talks about problems but it will also offer solutions. Some of them are just suggestions from a very ordinary middle-aged punter, but some of the advice will come with a lot more weight, wisdom and authority, because it comes from the Bible. If the Bible is a new idea for you, good—it's well worth the effort. If you've been reading the Bible for a while, you won't need to be convinced it is worth listening to.

Groundhog day

Chapter 1

Midlife—the good news

In general, life is better than it ever has been and if you think that in the past there was some golden age of pleasure and plenty to which you would, if you were able, transport yourself, let me say one single word: "Dentistry".

PJ O'Rourke, *All the trouble in the world*[1]

Let's start with some good news. If you're reading this book, and you are in 'midlife', you have a lot to be thankful for. Here are three things for certain:

Firstly, you have already had a long life compared to most people who have lived and died on the planet. Even as I write this in 2007 the average life expectancy at birth for a male in Liberia is just 37.9 years.[2] The average life expectancy at birth for a person in the first century Roman Empire was less than thirty years, and possibly a lot less.[3] So cheer up! In the ancient world most blokes had to have their midlife crises and go through adolescence at the same time. Asking 'Where has my life gone?' while learning to shave would have been pretty tough!

Secondly, unless this book has sold better than the publishers expected, you are probably living in Australia, or at least a rich westernised country—with all the benefits this brings. We live in a country with access to medicine, surgery, anaesthetic, clean water, more than enough food, shelter, peace, and safety. This is an age of wealth. In Australia we are now three times richer than we were in the 1950s.[4] The fact that it still doesn't seem enough is a problem we'll look at later.

In the ways in which things can be measured with numbers or graphs or dollars, life is good!

Thirdly, if you are reading this book, you have been educated. You can read. Or this is now an audio book and you've got access to a CD or MP3 player.

So, it's a fair assumption that we have things to be thankful for. For most of us, there have been and still are so many good things in life. How long is it since you took the time to remember those things? How long is it since you sat down on your own, with an old photo album? My guess is a lot of men never do it. You might want to try it sometime because it's good for the soul. There are generally more photos taken at weddings and parties than funerals, and this is because we usually take photos of the good things in life. Give it a go. You might find there are some healthy reminders of what your life has given you.

Glory days
Well time slips away and leaves you nothing mister,
but boring stories of glory days,
glory days they'll pass you by, glory days,
in the wink of a young girl's eye
glory days

Bruce Springsteen, *Glory Days*

Can you remember the times when you felt most alive?

Most of us have felt the elation of being in love; the heart rate that quickened each time we saw her. The smile that lit up the room. The elation when she said 'yes'—she would go out with us. We can remember the first time we kissed her, when she said 'yes' to marriage and the sense that you would live happily ever after.

If you have a child, how cool was it when they were born, and you held your wife's hand, maybe not sure what to do, but so proud of her? And then you probably cried like a beauty queen as you held this little person for the first time. Born tiny and helpless and yet with both hands already firmly around your heart, a grip most of us will never pry free. It's twenty-three years now since my first daughter (Amy) was born on March 14, at about 5:30 am. I still remember nursing her in the delivery room. My wife Kathy had drifted off, half asleep following the long labour (and a lot of happy gas), and as I held Amy she didn't cry or wriggle, she just looked up at me without blinking, with beautiful Eurasian eyes the colour of Club chocolate. The colour of those eyes hasn't changed. Often as I look at her, twenty-three years is like twenty-three minutes.

We all have moments in our lives that we remember. Those of us who are parents remember the joy that it was to see these little ones grow up—our hearts squeezed again as we saw first steps, first words. For some of us the joy of seeing girls blossom into young women, or boys eat and grunt their way into manhood, is a treasure we carry.

Have you known the satisfaction of graduating after a long time of study—holding the certificate or diploma or degree in your hand? You may think back to your first big job interview, when you cracked it. Or when you received the news that you had won that scholarship. Remember your first pay packet, or the first car you owned? For me it was a 1960s EJ Holden that did 0-100 in just 15 minutes!

Maybe it's the times when you really nailed it at work. When the boss called you in and spoke about your future, and what you might achieve. Can you remember the satisfaction of a promotion, or maybe your own office for the first time?

When you think of feeling most alive, your mind might drift to concerts you have been to that lifted you above the ordinary and into realms that felt positively spiritual. For me, that would have to be Bruce Springsteen at the Sydney Cricket Ground. Not everyone shares my love for the Boss, but perhaps for you it was Andrea Bocelli or Frank Sinatra; Eric Clapton or The Stones; the Three Tenors or U2.

For some of us it may have been academic triumphs, a PhD or a Masters involving years of effort. What about victories on the sporting field? A grand final or match-winning try; your first century, or a hat trick, or goal? Those are the times when you felt strong and alive.

Or it may have been 'being there'. I was there the night in 1994, when George Gregan made *that tackle* on Geoff Wilson to stop the All Blacks winning the Test Match. Where were you in 2000 when Cathy Freeman won the 400 metres at the Sydney Olympics?

You might have memories of a road trip with your mates, windows down and AC/DC pumping. (I know I'm beginning to show my true colours). Perhaps you are thinking of a motor bike trip through the mountains; watching the sun rise sitting on a surfboard at Byron, or Bells; holding a beach rod at dusk as you landed the big one. Standing on a mountaintop, or watching the sun set over Santorini with that special girl.

The strange thing is, when life is really good, when our relationships are good, and the people we love, love us, when we feel fit and strong, that's when we feel that this is the way life was meant to be. Why do we feel that? What are we in touch with in those moments?

Life can be and often is great. But, underneath as time goes by, for many of us there is a growing feeling of unease or sometimes even desperation. This angst grows as the late 30s become 40s or early 50s. Where does that feeling come from? Many men speak of it. Many more feel it. What is it about midlife that brings this on? And what does it look like when it arrives?

Is it that something changes with marriage and family, with work, and fun, and study and sport and music? What happens? In Chapter 2 we'll look at what happens when midlife arrives and why it's not an easy time for men. My guess is that if you've read this far you have probably felt this already.

By the way, make sure you read on past Sections 1 and 2. There is good news later in the book, but if you stop reading after the first part, you may find yourself looking for a tall building, and not because you feel like Superman!

Chapter 2

The midlife train arrives

Life is an inherently disappointing experience for most human beings.

Bob Carr, Premier of NSW, 1999[5]

Now and then my brother has a day's work in the Sydney CBD. He works as a carpenter, and I am in an office in the city. We arrange a coffee at about 11:00am. He's 45, with three teenage kids, a mortgage, and works long hours. My usual question is, 'So, what's happening mate?' His usual response is 'You know, (a shrug of the shoulders, a wry smile) "Groundhog Day".'[6] I nod knowingly, and roll my eyes. I feel his pain.

So many men seem to experience it. For some it happens quickly—almost overnight. For others it's a slow drawn-out but undeniably growing feeling. However we arrive there, it happens. One day we look at ourselves and our lives and wonder, 'What has happened to me? How did I get here? Where are the dreams I once had?' We feel trapped in 'groundhog' day. As the T-shirt says: 'same sh_t, different day'. We live with stress and the pressure to perform. We worry about the future or coping with work or financial pressure. We worry about someone twenty years younger taking our job, or worse, ending up our boss.

We live with boredom and stress. If stress is worry about coping and getting through the day or the week, and boredom is about the same thing repeating again and again, how is it that we can manage to be stressed and bored all at the same time? Somehow we do.

If your head is nodding at this point, welcome to midlife. Bill Clinton said 'when memories overtake dreams, you know you've grown old'. Midlife is when we start to notice that beginning to happen, and say 'wait a minute, that can't be happening, I'm not ready! I haven't done enough stuff yet!'

So how do you know if you're in midlife?

It's a bit like falling in love. You'll know when you get there. But there are definitely some clues that I have run up against. Here are just a few:

Grumpiness. I seem to have been grumpy so much in the last few years. It's nothing serious, just low level background grumpy—but with good cause. For example, is it just me or is so much of the new music these days just rubbish? Rap isn't music at all, and not only that, they take perfectly good songs from the 70s or 80s and do remixes of them. As far as I can tell, 'remix' is just another way of saying you are going to murder a song by doubling the speed and putting in a drum machine.

I was at the gym this morning and heard the remix of *Eye of the Tiger*, the theme from Rocky III or was it IV, it doesn't matter—it made me background low level cranky. The music was so loud in the gym—the veins on my baldy head were pulsing. I went and very politely asked the girl at the front desk if she could change the music or change the volume. I was really polite, but the look she gave me didn't say 'sure you fine young athlete'. The look she gave me made me think—welcome to midlife.

Baldness. I was going bald before I could grow a beard, and have been shaving my head for eight or nine years now. I decided if I'm going to be bald I might as well do it with attitude!—just lather up and shave off every thing except my eyebrows. One advantage is it is much easier applying sun block, and I'm so far gone that hair replacement was never a temptation.

Presents. Another sign of midlife is that the presents you get for birthdays and Christmas begin to change. You know that you are at least *heading* for midlife when you not only receive socks and underpants as presents, but you actually like getting them. By midlife hair grows everywhere—nose, ears, back of the neck—except where you actually want it to. Your eyebrows go feral. I'm seriously thinking about asking for a nose hair trimmer for Christmas this year.

The hard truth

Like a lot of men my age, when I talk about midlife I tend to make jokes about it. But there is a serious side to all of this. The truth is that there are aspects of midlife that aren't funny, and actually represent a lot of pain and loss.

I reckon Thoreau was right when he spoke of men living lives of quiet desperation. The desperation is real for many men, and so is the quietness. We might not talk about it—perhaps we don't have anyone to talk to—but it is there.

In 1994, when Steve Biddulph published his book *Manhood*, it touched a chord with many people. He wrote of the plight of men today:

> Most men don't have a life. What we have
> instead is a big act, kept up for protection. Early
> in our adult lives, we pick up one of several
> standard masks—hard worker, cool dude, good
> bloke, tough guy, sensitive new man. And then

things are fine. 'It's cool'. 'She'll be right'.
Underneath, though, there is often a profound
loneliness. Pretending, and having a life, are not
the same thing.[7]

Biddulph's argument in the early 90s as he encouraged 'the men's movement', is that we have forgotten how to be men, and especially lost contact with men of other generations whose wisdom and love we need. His summary of how so many lives end up is:

Our marriages fail, our kids hate us, we die from
stress and on the way we destroy the world.[8]

Apart from that, things are going pretty well.

Biddulph suggests that it's often not until midlife that the cracks begin to show, or be felt.

This is what is happening with men today.
Problems with health, marriage, parenthood,
ability to make friends and failure at work are
some of the ways they are alerted to deep holes
in their being. As young men we act cocky and
cheerful but as the pressures of life stack up, our
deficiencies become more obvious.[9]

The midlife crisis is laughed about at times, but what is it? I suspect it is simply a reaction from a desperate man, who feels trapped, bored, stifled, and helpless, and senses his life is ebbing away.

What brings this pressure to men's lives? There is a conspiracy of many parts, working together to make midlife a difficult time for us. 'Difficult' may be an understatement; frustrating, boring, crushing, joyless might capture it better. Let's have look at some of those conspirators. We'll start with some of the big ones first.

Chapter 3

The conspiracy

Death

It's not that I'm afraid to die, I just don't want to be there when it happens.

Woody Allen

The clock is ticking.

By midlife we realise we will die. This is not rocket science. Every child from an early age knows that every human dies—I am a human, therefore I will die. But when we are young this is an academic fact that somehow doesn't apply to us.

As I think back to being a kid in a country town, I had lots of elderly relatives. My two great aunts (sisters of my two grandparents) used to live in the same old house. They would pay my brother and me to come around and do gardening. I must admit there were different agendas operating. For my brother and me most of the time was spent chasing their chooks around the jungle that was the chook run, and in hindsight I realise the two old dears just wanted an excuse to have their nephews visit and to give us money and lollies we didn't deserve. It always seemed to me that the aunties, old and wrinkled and slow, were from a different planet. Certainly they were not from the same species as my brother and me. We would never look like them, or be old like them. And so even when they died by the time I was in my early twenties, it was sad, but it never really touched me.

It is a different story now as I watch my parents age, I see my Dad become an old man—that's me in just twenty-two years. It's not fun.

As we hit midlife we see death coming for others, and we feel it coming for us. Life is a series of transitions—within our tribe—eighteenth and twenty-first birthdays, weddings, christenings, and divorces, and then as we arrive at midlife, funerals. We lose our parents, or if our parents live on, our friends start burying their parents. The loss of a parent is more than grief. It is a reminder of our own mortality. As one of my friends said after his father died, 'You see your father die, the older generation goes, and then it's your turn to step up and stand at the edge'.

As we get older we begin to lose our friends as well. I've seen three of my mates buried in the last few years—one from a heart attack, one from cancer, and another from a brain tumour. We step closer to the edge.

Recently I met a man who lived a few suburbs away from me. He was in his eighties and had lived in the same suburb, in the same street, and worked close by, for more than forty years. He was desperately lonely, as his wife had died a few months before. I remember thinking, 'why doesn't he have support from his mates, after forty or fifty years of friendship?' Then later I realised he had outlived all his mates. He had buried them over the last thirty years. This slow process of goodbyes begins in midlife.

By the time we get to mid thirties we can hear a small voice telling us that we won't live forever. By the time we get to our forties and fifties the small voice has become a megaphone, reminding us daily of our own mortality. It's a voice we notice when our eyes don't work as well and skin starts sagging on our elbows, or under chins, or our foreheads start growing through our hair. It's a voice that is in our ear when we notice we are starting to look like our fathers—old. The voice is often loudest the morning after unplanned sporting contests with younger males, at BBQs, and family gatherings. It seems the male mind is slower to grasp the aging process than the male body.

Loss

I wonder if it is actually possible to get any sympathy for the pain of aging. Your peers don't really want to talk about it. They are going through it themselves. Those who are older have even bigger things to worry about, and besides they can't hear that well anyway. Maybe the young will care? Just try talking to your kids or other people twenty years younger about aches and pains or about your athletic ability in the glory days, and see how long their attention span is. Even if they stay in the same room or keep looking at you, the 'screen-saver' will be on in their head before you have finished two sentences.

Let's face it—our aging is boring, even to us. You're bored with this paragraph already. But aging hurts and we carry around a sense of grief for what we are losing. We can feel time slipping away.

Health

Most young men don't have a regular General Practitioner, but as midlife comes on we need to find a doctor for regular checkups. The major criteria for selection will be that the doctor has small and delicate hands, or at least short fingers. As comedian Billy Connelly says, when he reached middle-age, his doctor became far less interested in the front of him! In your teens the 'race cams' inside the cars at Mt Panorama were exciting. In middle-age this is replaced by 'butt-cam', which is worrying to say the least.

Last year, because of family history and a few other symptoms you don't want to know about, I ended up visiting a friend of mine who is a colorectal surgeon. The first thing I noticed as I sat in his examination room was that in the twenty years I'd known him, I'd never realised he had probably the biggest hands I had ever seen: ten huge, hairy sausages with finger nails.

As I lay on the examination table in the foetal position, with my pants around my ankles, knees near my chin, trying to look dignified, I thought, 'Welcome to the joys of midlife!'

Snap went the rubber glove.

Body slowing down

As we grow older it takes more effort and discipline to stay in shape. In fact our shape will change regardless of what we do. Exercise and diet become more and more important. Dr John Best has written a chapter in this book on this issue (see Appendix A). Turn to it when you are ready. He has some really good advice to offer men on health and exercise in midlife.

The irony is, the harder we exercise in middle age, (and exercise we should) the more regularly the reminders come that we can't do what we used to. We're just not as fast or strong as we once were and injuries take much longer to heal. Our glory days become more glorious as we succumb to the adage, 'The older I get the better I was'.

Food becomes an issue. When we were kids most of us could eat what ever we wanted and it didn't matter. Now it's not just the quantity of food we're supposed to be disciplined about, but the kind of food we eat.

Here's another news flash. With midlife we get tired. We can't work the way we used to. We begin to slow down physically. Mates of mine who are tradesmen start feeling the days are longer and the loads are heavier. Even those of us who work in offices find the mental work gets harder. Maybe we just carry more responsibility. Maybe we are just getting older.

I work in an office, and an average day including travel is 7:45am to about 7:00pm. When I get home I'm brain dead, and my emotional tank is empty. I eat dinner, organise a shirt for the next day and before long I'm thinking about heading for bed.

Time

One of the ironies of midlife is that the days may get longer but the years get shorter. Time seems to speed up. I've heard different theories as to why this is (I won't bore you with them as time is short). As a kid I can remember Christmas would just never arrive, but now Christmases speed past like picket posts.

You know the saying about a woman's 'biological clock ticking'—the pressure a woman feels as her child bearing years are passing by. Strangely men feel a biological clock ticking too—the passing of physical health, strength, even physical attractiveness. But we aren't allowed to talk about it. Try talking about feeling your biological clock ticking and see how your mates react. Somewhere we cross a line, where cute, young, female shop assistants, call us 'Sir' and speak to us like we are their fathers. Pleasant retail service is nice, but it makes the shoulders stoop, as we realise, 'She sees me in her Dad's generation'.

Speaking of Dads we start to not only look like our Dads, but act like them as well. The other day I found myself wanting to get hold of a kid and give him a hair cut. My habit of wanting everything labelled and neat is something I have inherited from my Dad.

Physical changes associated with midlife are a worry. But perhaps more serious is the hole left in our lives by what hasn't happened. It is this issue of lost dreams that we turn to next.

Chapter 4

What hasn't happened

I knew I was getting old when I finally accepted that I probably wasn't ever going to be picked in the Australian cricket team.

Wil Anderson—Comedian

As the clock ticks on, we are aware of what is happening physically, but we also start to become aware of what hasn't happened. What hasn't happened for so many of us, is our dreams. We become aware that we will not change the world. The dreams we had are not going to happen after all.

Steve Biddulph says it like this:

> Young men in their late teens and twenties are cocky. They have an optimism that is charming but shallow—since it has never been tested. They are inclined to think they are invincible. Eventually though all men learn that not everything works out in this life. The mid-thirties seem to be the time that this often happens. The trigger can be anything. Perhaps a baby is stillborn. Or your wife stops loving you. A once sturdy father shrivels and dies before

your eyes. A lump becomes cancerous. A car accident smashes up your body. Or your carefully built career tumbles like a pack of cards. Suddenly there is shame, error and grief all around you. Welcome to the ashes.[10]

Robert Bly in *Iron John* adds to the description:

Despite our Disneyland culture, some men around thirty-five or forty will begin to experience ashes privately, without ritual, even without old men. They begin to notice how many of their dreams have turned to ashes. A young man in high school dreams that he will be a race driver, mountain climber, he will marry Miss America, he will be a millionaire by thirty, he will get a prize in physics by thirty-five, he will be an architect and build the tallest building ever. He will get out of this hick town and live in Paris. He will have fabulous friends... and by thirty-five, all these dreams are ashes.[11]

Even if your fantasies as a young man weren't as grandiose as these, most of us had dreams of what we would be, what we would achieve, and places we would go. Middle-age means coming to terms with the fact that many of these dreams are just not going to happen. When we were younger we could still think... 'one day', but not any more. We will never be a rock star, a famous sportsman, a big business man, and now time is running out. Life has become ordinary, mundane and predictable. Our dreams have died the death of a thousand responsibilities or obligations.

Shrinking possibilities

Men past forty
Get up nights, Look out at city lights
And wonder
Where they made the wrong turn
And why life is so long

Ed Sissman[12]

As time goes by our options narrow. In fact as our past stretches out behind us, our future options seem to narrow before us. We face shrinking possibilities. 'If only' are two very tough words to live with.

In our twenties we can leave one job or career and move to another, no problem. I've had friends who have done exactly that. One man I knew from university trained as an optometrist and then in his late twenties retrained as a doctor. Another bloke I know was a policeman until he was thirty and then went to Bible College to become an Anglican minister. The younger we are the more options we have with what we do for work or where we will live—in fact more options with all parts of our lives.

Then one day we wake up middle-aged and with our options gone. We are simply too old to retrain. It's too hard to study, or new jobs/careers won't take us. I know someone who through a series of circumstances found himself looking at a new career. He is a bright guy who writes well and tried to get into an ad agency as a copywriter. He was told at the interview that he was too old for the job. He is thirty-five!

Many of us live in fear of losing our jobs. In a society obsessed with youth it can be very hard for a middle-aged man to find work. It is a hard thing for some of us to be reporting to someone younger, maybe significantly younger than we are. And so we may hate our jobs but battle on without the option of looking elsewhere. We feel stuck in, if not a prison, then at least a cul-de-sac. There is no way out.

Matthew is a carpenter in the building industry. He is good at his trade. When he started as a teenager, he was as strong as a horse, and loved the physical work. Now the same work for almost thirty years has become boring. At 45 it's boring and tiring. But there's no way out, he's too old to become a fireman or join the police; too old to become a pilot which he'd love to be. So he gets up each morning and goes to work. He starts each day bored and finishes bored and tired. And he probably has twenty years to go until he can retire. How does Matthew get up and go to work each morning for the next twenty years?

Disillusionment

There are two sources of unhappiness in life. One is not getting what you want; the other is getting it.

George Bernard Shaw

Of course not everyone deals with the disillusionment of not achieving goals and dreams. For some the dream becomes a reality, but fails to live up to its promise. They hit middle-age and still ask the question 'Is this all there is?' At the peak of his success writer Jack Higgins was asked what he now knows that he wished he had known as a younger man. He replied, 'I wish I had known that when you get to the top there is nothing there.'[13]

So here's the cheery summary of middle-age. The biological clock is ticking, not on child bearing but on wrinkles, baldness, arthritis—and if we're lucky enough to last, we can look forward to a slow and inevitable death. Also as life stretches out behind us, the options in front of us narrow.

We may well feel that we have slowly, brick by brick, built ourselves a wall that we live behind and cannot escape from. Let's look at some of the bricks in the wall in the next chapter. Later we'll look at some of the wrong ways blokes try to knock down the wall.

Chapter 5

The bricks in the wall

Now all them things that seemed so important,
well Mister they vanished right into the air.
Now I just act like I don't remember,
Mary acts like she don't care

Bruce Springsteen, *The River*

Marriage

In the wall of midlife bricks, marriage is such a key one, that I will dedicate a whole chapter to it, before discussing some of the others.

What goes wrong with marriages? We've all been at the weddings. The couple both seem like volunteers don't they? People spend the equivalent of the national debt of an African nation and one partner spends a year planning, so they can both volunteer. Weddings are so bubbly and happy. It's all smiles and photos. But what does the future so often hold?

Here's some alternative wedding vows...

- And do you '...name ...and ...name...'
  promise to slowly grow apart and not really
  talk to each other within a few years.

- Will you lose any romantic love for one another, and just drop into a business partnership.

- Will you, *husband,* throw yourself into your work so much that you aren't really welcome at home even when you want to come back?

- Will you, *husband,* stop making the effort to engage with her emotionally, so she doesn't feel like 'engaging' physically?

- Will you, *wife,* shut down physically in a few years? Will you lose interest in sex and when you do have sex with him, do it as one more housework job for the day, or not at all?

- Will one or both of you stop looking after yourselves physically? (i.e. get fat and flabby)

- Will you speak badly about one another and belittle one another in front of other people? Will you stop praising or complementing one another completely?

- Will you stay together really only because of the children?

- Will you decide it's all too hard and separate with all the heartache that brings?

If those were the vows couples took, no one would get married, and yet this is a picture of where so many marriages end up. What goes wrong? There are many theories and I don't claim to be an expert, but for what it's worth, here is what I think happens:

We get busy, tired, and selfish, and we don't cope with transitions. Busy, tired and selfish aren't so hard to understand, but what do I mean by transitions? If you have kids, you can look forward to five different marriages. I didn't say five different wives, although sometimes it may seem like it. It depends on the age of your kids and the different pressures you are likely to face at different times of your life. Here are some of them:

Double income no kids

That's the easy part. You really should be able to get on well together at this stage. You share your lives but have a degree of independence. You can travel light, sleep in, spend money from a high combined income, eat out, go to parties, and still be selfish young adults together.

New born to toddlers

All of a sudden your whole life is turned upside down. You have no sleep, no sex, and your wife has become a mother—tired, overwhelmed and focused on anything but you. Negotiating roles becomes an intricate exercise in diplomacy. The whole of life revolves around what the five-kilo dictator wants. It now takes about one hour to get ready to leave the house as a family. You spend much of your time changing nappies, and walking around shopping centres with prams the size of a small family car.

Middle kids

The kids are a bit older. The sports car has been replaced by a people mover, and you spend most Saturdays making polite conversation with strangers at children's birthday parties and trying not to strangle soccer mums from the other team.

Teenagers

These years are a lottery. We'll discuss these in more detail next chapter, but suffice to say, you need a united front at this critical stage which can put pressure not only on your relationship with your kids, but on your marriage as well. Problems with teenagers can drive a wedge between married couples.

The empty nest

This stage brings its own challenges. You and your wife are living together in the home by yourselves for the first time in many years. The busy and noisy house is strangely quiet. If you have neglected the relationship in the intervening years this can be a time where the things you had in common when you first got together are just a distant memory.

The key is being able to relate to your wife through all the various stages, and making the marriage a priority. There will always be new reasons not to talk to each other properly, new opportunities to withdraw into our shells, and new and varied things to give priority to ahead of the marriage.

No one plans to let their marriage fade away, but we neglect our marriages at our peril, and to the detriment of our kids as well.

Sex

Sex in midlife is not always what we might hope it to be. Nigel Marsh in *Fat, Forty and Fired*, comments on a 'friend's' (i.e. his) sex life:

> (His belief was that he needed to first ascertain where sex ranked in his wife's priorities.)

> 'Sweetheart, is sex as important to you, say, as a holiday away?' he started.

'No? Okay how about a weekend away?' he continued.

'No? That's fine, that's fine. A good meal?' he suggested.

'No? No problem, it's important you're honest. Does it rank above a glass of wine?' he asked.

This line of questioning went on until—and I'm not making this up—he got down to 'cleaning the oven'. At this stage he got into a serious debate about whether sex was something she looked forward to more or less than cleaning the oven. She eventually settled on an equal ranking. Another friend of mine once told me in deep depression that his marriage was like 'running a kindy with a roommate you used to date'. Nice.[14]

When I was working, one of my clients had once opened up after a few drinks. 'It's always a wearing down process, Nigel. I make a move and she rejects me. I wait a few days then suggest it again. She rejects me again. I feel resentful and hurt. She feels guilty and pressured. I wait a few more days. Women in the street, newsreaders on TV and gargoyles on the top of buildings start to look strangely appealing. We argue, I shout, she cries. We make up, and she says something like, "O go on then you big bear, I'll let you". Trouble is, I don't want to be 'let'. I'd like her to want to. I don't want it to be a reward for good behaviour or Olympic patience. It makes me feel dirty and

ashamed that I want to get my end away.
I'd like to be surprised and delighted by my
sex life, not depressed and bored.'[15]

So in midlife, if we are not careful, our sex life slows down or stops. There comes a time when it's easier for a man to simply shut down sexually than to get knocked back again. The pain of getting knocked back is too great, each time it happens self-esteem suffers. Dr Amelia Haines has written on middle-aged men and sex in Appendix B. Turn to it when you want to (if you haven't already).

Divorce

With the divorce rate approaching forty-five per cent it is a fair bet that some readers will be divorced. With that comes pain, broken relationships, shattered families and heartache. And here's the problem—midlife and divorced, often means that we have kids we love and want to get access to but can't. It also means being financially shattered, with assets divided, and having to pay child support as well as live somewhere yourself. One man I know spends his whole week waiting and planning how to spend time with his kids on the weekends, and his ex-wife makes it difficult for him.

For some men who haven't married, middle-age means the feeling that the window of opportunity to marry is closing. The older we get the less likely it is that we will marry and have children. Being single can bring great freedom. You go where you want when you want. You can use your own telephone and shower when you want. But loneliness can be a crushing problem.

Loneliness within marriage might be even more tragic. Some more of the 'bricks' of the midlife wall will be discussed in the next chapter.

Chapter 6

Some more bricks in the midlife wall

Oh yeah life goes on
Long after the thrill of livin is gone

John Cougar Mellancamp, *Jack and Diane*

Family

It can be hard work being Dad whatever the stage of family life. Men are marrying later, and having kids later. In midlife we can be at any stage of family life. I have one friend who is a first time Dad at forty-three and another friend who was a grandfather at forty-five.

The expectations now seem so much higher for fathers than when I was a kid.

My Dad was a good Dad. He came to see me play sport a few times, when there was something big on. I remember it was special. He turned up now and then for stuff at school. If I bought home a good report card from school, he said 'Good work mate', and that was about it.

It's different today. We need to be at sport to watch our kids every week for their psychological health. We now have 'serial killer events' in our family, where we joke that if we as parents miss this event (speech night, or sport or what ever), you can guarantee our child will grow up to be a serial killer. Such psychological damage will be done that in twenty years time, when dismembered human body parts are found in their freezer, no jury will convict—with the defence, 'My dad missed my Year 8 hockey game'!

If you're a midlife Dad there's a good chance you're spending much of your weekends driving kids places, watching sport, being interested, meeting other parents at kid's functions. You do really have to jump in and help. How can we expect our wives to drive all the kids to lessons for three musical instruments each, a couple of sports, a second language session, and maths tutoring? In the middle of it all, some of us occasionally think—what about a life for me?

Teenagers

Parenting teenagers is difficult. Firstly they may well be bigger than you now, (discipline changes when you're looking up at them). You lose your television, your telephone (although mobiles have helped here) and your shower.

Dad often ends up coming home from work and walking into refereeing fights between mum and teenage kids, 'I've asked him all day, can you tell him to do "x"?' 'Dad can't you get her off my back?'. Sometimes poor old Dad can manage a 'Solomon' and sort it out. But pretty regularly it's like throwing two cats in a bag, shaking it up and then sticking your head in. Not a lot of fun.

And in many ways it is a lottery as to how your teenage children will respond when they hit these turbulent years. I've known kids from troubled homes who have gone through teenage years as mature responsible young adults. Others known to me from what you might call 'good stable homes' have hit teen years and a transformation has occurred. In fact it's more like an alien abduction, that leaves you wondering 'Where is the nice kid that was here a few months ago, and who's this monster the aliens left behind?' You might find you and your wife are running a drop-in centre for a few years until, one day, the kids you got to know and love magically return as if nothing has ever happened.

Letting them go—as young adults—is difficult. They naturally look forward and out, not back toward us. It's natural we have to let them go. Seeing them grow up and become more and more independent is good in many ways, and sad as you watch them go and wonder what is the next stage of life for me?

Parents

One of the joys of midlife, is that we can worry about our kids and our parents at the same time. One writer has called this being part of the sandwich generation. As our parents get older, the worry about how they will look after themselves in terms of care and finances becomes very real. Where will they live, who will care for them? And they aren't always cooperative, are they!

We feel an obligation to care for our parents and rightly so. We should look after them. But it is one more obligation we feel. We can reach the point where we can feel a failure as a son and a father all at once.

The weight of expectations

Put together these expectations of marriage, kids, parents, a job and all that comes with it, and the weight of responsibility can feel crushing. So many commitments and responsibilities can gradually suck the joy out of life.

Many men in midlife feel exactly that—the joy has been sucked out of life.

Do you notice how often banks and people in the 'retirement planning industry' are pushing the idea of having fun and leaving responsibility behind. I've seen lots of ads that show the late middle-aged couple loading up a backpack, grabbing a Eurail pass and leaving their grown up kids behind. One bank advertisement expressed the sentiment like this:

> Do you remember when your son rebelled by
> buying a motor bike—retirement is payback
> time.

That may be all right for baby boomers intent on 'SKIN'ing[16] their kids, but what about those of us who have fifteen or twenty years of work to go?

Many men I talk to are bored and asking 'Where has the fun gone?'

Loneliness

The sense I get is it that many men in midlife are lonely. We may not admit it, but many men have very few or no friends. And the problem seems to get worse as we get older. As Jerry Sienfeld asked... 'Why is it that when you're 8 years old... if a kid stops his bike outside your house you immediately want to be friends, but by the time you're thirty-five the sign has gone up—"Sorry we're not hiring"?'

Some writers put this down to men being naturally competitive. This innate competitiveness stems from a life-long search for approval, and leads us to constantly compare ourselves with other men and measure our worth and the worth of others based on status, income, what type of car we drive and the house we live in.

Such competitiveness discourages healthy friendships and it may be part of the problem, but I think there are other reasons. Men are shy. Men are busy. Men are less likely to admit they are lonely, and perhaps this is pride, or perhaps it's simply a lack of social skills. Or it could be that a lot of blokes only talk when they have something to say. Women talk face to face, men talk side by side. We talk to each other as we do stuff, like fishing or watching football or playing pool.

There is also the fact that beyond work and looking after our families and keeping the house in order there simply isn't time to do things with friends. After years of this, men can find themselves isolated and alone.

The picture I have been building is a fairly depressing one, and while you may not have gone through anything as grim as this, I'm sure you'll have been nodding your head to at least some, if not most of the points I have raised.

But where do we go for answers? In the next chapter, I will introduce you to what I think may hold the key to solving the midlife blues.

Chapter 7

Ancient wisdom

What does man gain from all his labour at which he toils under the sun?

(Ecclesiastes 1:3)

What I hope to do in writing these chapters is to encourage middle-aged men to put distractions aside and begin to ask, perhaps for the first time, 'What's life really about? What matters? What has real value? What lasts? Why are we here?'

There is an ancient text, written almost 3000 years ago that feels to me like it could have been written yesterday; and it addresses these very questions. I reckon this little book, buried in the Old Testament part of the Bible, is relevant to every stage of life, but if there is a book that speaks powerfully to midlife, it has to be this one. The book is *Ecclesiastes*.

Ecclesiastes

Right off the bat Ecclesiastes focuses on the problem of finding meaning and purpose in life. The writer asks the question... what gives life meaning? What has real value, what will last? And he will not accept any easy answers or be sidetracked with distractions.

No one is sure who the author of Ecclesiastes is, but many think it could have been Solomon, the son of King David, who reigned about 1000 BC. Solomon was the richest, most prosperous King of Israel. You've probably heard the expression 'the wisdom of Solomon', which is a reference to this King.

Ecclesiastes never actually identifies Solomon as the author. It is possible a subsequent author wrote *through the eyes* of Solomon to make the point about what gives life meaning and purpose. But for convenience sake I will just call him Solomon. Ecclesiastes is worth a whole study in itself, but here we will just seek to hit some of the high notes and see how they particularly relate to men in midlife.

Human ants

Solomon begins by looking at our world. (See Ecclesiastes 1:1–11 in the endnotes)[17]. He focuses on the big picture and says 'What's it all about?' I can imagine him, scratching his greying head as he grasps for purpose and significance. 'Generations come and generations go, but the earth remains forever', he says. The point being we are so insignificant in terms of time—we're here for such a short while—and despite a very successful life, Solomon feels the weight of this problem.

At Uluru—the local aboriginal guides call the tourists 'ants' and it's a little hard to work out why until you go to the visitors centre where they show a film of the tourist buses arriving. In fast motion all the tourists get out quickly and swarm around and then some swarm over the rock and swarm back and take their photos and get in the bus and then they are gone. Uluru stays there and always has and always will. I thought it was fascinating—

generations come, generations go, we are here for five minutes and then we are gone.

Early in the book Solomon turns from our insignificance in terms of time, to the monotony of the world.

> The sun rises and the sun sets, and hurries back
> to where it rises. The wind blows to the south
> and turns to the north; round and round it goes,
> ever returning on its course (Ecclesiastes 1:5–6).

He's not celebrating the reliability of the created order, which other parts of the Bible talk about, but the monotony of life.

He follows this by lamenting that nothing is ever accomplished, and later, that nothing is ever truly new. If you see the world that way how do you react? Many of us can relate to Solomon's thinking.

> All things are wearisome, more than one can say.
> The eye never has enough of seeing, nor the ear
> its fill of hearing (Ecclesiastes 1:8).

The point is, all things are wearisome, and you can get bored with anything. Amusement parks are exciting places, but have you ever looked at the staff who run them? They are not amused are they? Not after a few days. They are totally bored. On the 1999 Stewart family vacation, we drove up to the Northern Territory and I paid money for a fishing guide to take me barramundi fishing. I still didn't catch a barra but I did get a few salmon and it was a great day.

Here we were out in the middle of nowhere trying to catch barramundi, and if you love fishing you'll understand why this is so great. The guide I was with had taken on the job because he loved fishing and yet, as I was all excited trying to catch a barra, guess what? He was bored out of his brain.

All things are wearisome, more than one can say.

Meaninglessness

After a while you get to a certain age and life becomes Groundhog Day and it's all relentlessly the same. This, says Solomon is the human problem.

We need to feel this emptiness before we can find the light. Solomon helps us out by providing something of a summary, both at the beginning and the end of Ecclesiastes, of the things we've been discussing so far.

> "Meaningless! Meaningless!" says the Teacher.
> "Utterly meaningless! Everything is
> meaningless" (Ecclesiastes 1:2).

That doesn't sound too promising but stay with me. What does he mean by that word meaningless? It is the Hebrew word 'Hebel' which means a vapour or breath, something that is there and then gone. He uses the word thirty-eight times in the book, so it is pretty much a key idea.

I was thinking about this as I drove my daughter to Hockey training recently. She had to be there at 7.00 am, and it was a cold winter's morning. We pulled up at the training field and as I looked out over the grass there was fog everywhere and she said 'I love the mist' as she crossed the road. The sun was shining on it, and it was there and pretty and bright and yet you couldn't grasp it and you couldn't hold on to it and in just a little while it was gone. That is what is meant by meaningless here. It's a vapour, it's nothing and then it's gone. It's also used to mean worthless or trivial.

Under the sun

What he is saying is that everything is meaningless, a vapour, it's transitory, nothing lasts, it's here and then it's gone. Everything is a mist that disappears. That's his starting point and then he sets out to argue this case for twelve chapters and with growing intensity. His argument is centred on a question that many men can relate to:

> What does man gain from all his labour at which
> he toils under the sun? (Ecclesiastes 1:3).

'Gain' is a commercial term, it is the idea of surplus, of what is left over, what remains. We would say 'For all our work, what's the bottom line?' He uses one little phrase here that is vitally important in understanding his entire argument—'under the sun'. He uses it twenty-seven times in the book. As far as I can work out what he means by this phrase 'under the sun' is—if our world was a closed system, if we didn't have any word from God, if God hadn't revealed himself, if all we had was common sense and our eyes to see, how would we make sense of this world, and what we see out there 'under the sun'?

Again and again he asks that question, 'What is the real value, the profit for all our work under the sun'. For all our busyness, all our activity; all our going to bed tired, waking up tired, rushing and commuting and so on, what is it all really worth?

His conclusion is that 'under the sun', without a word from God, if we live as if we are alone in the universe, then all our activity is meaningless. Perhaps it is this same sense that many of us feel when we hit midlife. We might have been able to distract ourselves for many years but now we long for something that really matters; something that lasts. This is what Ecclesiastes is all about.

Solomon is not a complete pessimist. He goes on to say some more positive things about life 'under the sun', but ultimately his findings are that meaninglessness is the human condition, and problem, 'under the sun'.

Importantly this is the start of Solomon's quest. He doesn't leave us with the idea of life being meaningless. He moves on. In the rest of Ecclesiastes Solomon sets out to see if he can find anything that gives life purpose—'under the sun'.

The search for answers

The search for answers

'Got a wife and kids in Baltimore jack
I went out for a ride and I never went back
Like a river that don't know where it's flowin
I took a wrong turn and I just kept goin.'

Bruce Springsteen, *Hungry Heart*

What I've tried to do up to now is paint a picture of what many men feel as they reach midlife. A common experience is that men feel trapped, slowly, brick by brick, being hemmed in to a life of obligation: of work that is hard, or boring, and yet feeling hand-cuffed to the job; of a marriage that isn't much fun anymore, and where they feel unappreciated; where sex is as exciting as housework but not as regular. Men can find themselves in family life feeling like they aren't doing a great job as a father, or that their kids don't think they are doing much of job as a dad. Midlife is where we see that the dreams we once had, have been slowly turned to ashes, where life is like Groundhog Day, and we are left asking 'Where's the fun?' Or as the writer of Ecclesiastes says, what do we do now that we have discovered everything is meaningless 'under the sun'?

There are a number of ways of responding to this situation and not all of them are good ones. Three pretty common responses are:

1. We can ignore the insights of midlife—ignore the biological clock; the lost dreams or the empty feeling of climbing the corporate ladder. We can simply bite down on the mouth guard and keep pushing on through Groundhog Day pretending we are okay.

or

2. We can try to smash down the wall of obligations by pulling the plug on relationships, and the people who rely on us. We can do our own thing; we can leave our marriages, and look for the freedom we experienced as young men.

or

3. We can give up, throw in the towel and withdraw from it all, because it's too hard. We can mow the lawn, watch television, do as our wives tell us and slowly die inside. I've seen a lot of blokes do this.

The pressure and struggle of midlife can lead to tired and desperate men making bad decisions. What kind of bad decisions do tired men make when it comes to midlife?

The cliché is to go out and buy a red sports car, or a Harley, which in themselves are fun and pretty harmless really, as long as you don't think this will solve anything.

The great damage occurs when we start looking for something that will be a quick fix.

Chapter 8

Pleasure, partying and possessions—a journey into hedonism

The worst kind of meaninglessness does not come from being weary of pain or poverty but from being weary of pleasure amid plenty.

Ravi Zacharias[18]

In Section I, I introduced you to Solomon, and suggested he has a bit to say when it comes to dealing with the pain of midlife. As he ponders the search for meaning and purpose, he says to himself, 'perhaps the answer is to be found in pleasure'—in hedonism—something our society is very well set up for.

At the beginning of Chapter 2 of Ecclesiastes, Solomon gives us a summary of his journey into hedonism. (See Ecclesiastes 2:1–11 in the endnotes.)[19]

> I thought in my heart, "Come now, I will test you
> with pleasure to find out what is good"
> (Ecclesiastes 2:1).

We need to remember that Solomon was a powerful and impressive King. He could pretty much ask for and receive whatever he wanted. When it came to pleasures in life, he didn't hold back, and his list of pleasurable diversions is impressive. He says he tried cheering himself with wine; he took on great projects and planted vineyards. He built houses and gardens and parks, and bought male and female slaves. He amassed piles of gold and other treasure and a harem— 'the delights of a man's heart' as he puts it. We learn from other parts of the Bible that Solomon had 1000 wives, and that he spent thirteen years building his palace. His was an extravagant reign that must have looked extremely impressive to observers. Solomon summarises this period of his life like this:

> I denied myself nothing my eyes desired; I refused
> my heart no pleasure (Ecclesiastes 2:10a).

But, strange as it may seem, that also proved to be meaningless.

> Yet when I surveyed all that my hands had done
> and what I had toiled to achieve, everything was
> meaningless, a chasing after the wind; nothing
> was gained under the sun (Ecclesiastes 2:11).

Solomon is not saying pleasure is a bad thing. He's not promoting the life of an ascetic—denying yourself pleasure, or flagellating yourself until you feel miserable. He's just saying pleasure is, in the end, meaningless ... a vapour—it disappears, it isn't substantial, it doesn't last. Pleasure is a bit like water in your hands. You can scoop up water and splash your face and it feels nice but you can't actually hold water in your hands, it just leaks out, you can't hold on to it and pleasure is like that. It's here and ... it's gone. It's transitory, not substantial, and therefore not the answer to life's biggest questions.

When we discussed Ecclesiastes 1 we talked about the way nothing ever changes—everything's the same. Solomon's problem is the same one many of us have today, and especially in midlife, because it is about then that the unsatisfying element of hedonism starts to really hit home.

Those with enormous amounts of money get to indulge themselves in lavish and extravagant ways—a little like Solomon did. I read a newspaper article about John B. Schultz, an architect who specialises in building outrageously expensive houses for outrageously rich people. Half the article is about the biggest house in England that cost a mere $70 million. By American standards this is small fry. In the United States, Larry Ellison takes on Bill Gates to the title of top cheese by building a bigger house than him.

In 2001 Gates announced that he was extending his $200 million home near Seattle, Washington—now you can see why he needs to expand. Gates has a wife and … one daughter! I guess he is a little short on room!

In response to Gates' little 'renovation' Larry Ellison replied with a $300 million Japanese style mansion in California—twice the size of the white house and complete with artificial lakes, waterfalls and 3800 tonnes of hand-chiselled Chinese granite for the retaining walls.

It's interesting that Gates and Ellison are both extending their homes. I wonder why they want to do it. Perhaps it is because when you have that much stuff, once you stop and look around at all that you have, you sense what Solomon sensed—that ultimately it doesn't deliver what it promises.[20] While these guys are extreme examples, the sense I get is that those of us with less money are no different. The obsession with home renovation in recent years tells me that the same 'problem' applies to the rest of us. We just can't seem to get enough stuff. We are no sooner finished one addition to our lives and we are thinking about the next.

Along with pleasure and wine and possessions, Solomon had also tried laughter in his quest to find out what is 'good'. One of the great ironies of life is that so often it is those with a brilliant sense of humour who use it to hide a sad heart. I think of some of the great funnymen of Hollywood, or of the most brilliant stand-up comics who turn out to be quite sad in real life. There is a proverb that says 'Even in laughter the heart may ache, and joy may end in grief' (Proverbs 14:13).

Laughter is to our lives what shock absorbers are to cars—it helps to make the ride a little more comfortable as we attempt to cope with the ironies and the pain of life.

I reckon Solomon probably really did enjoy all that he owned and had a good time for a little while, with his pleasures, possessions and projects, and a few good laughs. But in the end it was just empty, and did not satisfy. That's my experience as well and I expect it may be yours. Don't you sometimes look forward to getting something new—it might be a new car or particular article of clothing, or a bigger television and so you get it, and for fifteen minutes it's great! But even a new car becomes pretty ordinary fairly quickly. It just doesn't deliver in the way that we thought it would.

Many of us in midlife begin to find, like Solomon did, that the distractions of pleasure, possessions and projects are beginning to feel like 'chasing after the wind'. The answer, he concluded, must lie elsewhere.

Chapter 9
Money

The Police was a painful seven years. Everything you thought would make you happy was given to you, and then it did not make you happy. It's a horrible but also wonderful lesson to learn where real happiness comes from. It's not from success or money. It took me a while to find that out.

Rock musician *Sting* on his time in the band *The Police*[21]

A few years ago I saw big Arnie Schwarzenegger (before he was the Governator) on the Oprah Winfrey show. Here they were, Arnie and Oprah on the couch and she was going on about how Arnie was so successful as a film star and how he had become so rich. In the middle of talking about his money, Arnie said to her 'Oprah I have to tell you that I have found that money doesn't bring happiness. I now have $50 million and I am no happier than when I had $48 million!'

The big guy is really onto something there. He is making fun of the whole idea that says that money doesn't buy happiness. We don't believe that. We might say money doesn't buy happiness but my guess is most of us think, 'I'd like a truck load of it to find out for myself'.

Why is it that money is so powerful and seductive? I put it to you that money, and all that goes with it, answers two of our greatest needs—status and security. Sure, money might not be able to buy real, genuine heartfelt romantic love, but it does have a huge impact on how other people treat us (our status). Money delivers respect—people treat you differently if you are rich. You walk into a five star hotel, dressed appropriately, with a gold credit card in hand and you are treated very, very nicely, and it is very nice to be treated that way. So, there's a type of love that money provides, as well as many others things:

- Money gives you status and power. It is hard to argue with that one. People with money are given preferential treatment. Anyone who has climbed the stairs past the corporate boxes at the Rugby on the way to the nose-bleed seats will know what I am talking about.

- To a degree, money delivers safety—with money you can live in a better neighbourhood, you can drive a safer car, you can fly to Noosa rather then risk the Pacific Highway.

- Money shields you from unpleasant things, be that unpleasant temperatures through an air-conditioner, or unpleasant people through a security fence.

- Money delivers freedom; the more money you have the more able you are to do as you please, enjoy options in life.

- Money delivers pleasure; with money you are able to indulge yourself, whether that be the smell and feel of leather furniture, or ocean views, or exciting holidays.

- Money can provide better health in the sense that you can afford better medical treatment.

I recently heard from a man whom I see occasionally. Through a quirk of fate he looks like inheriting multiple millions of dollars in the next year or two. He said to me 'I know that money doesn't bring happiness, but when I think about this it makes my heart beat faster'. I suspect if I was in the same situation it might do that to me too. Our society has swallowed the line that money and possessions are what life is all about. We chase such things at full throttle with energy and purpose and determination. Deep down it is very hard to ignore the idea that money will bring happiness. But does it, or is it just like all good lies, a kind of a half-truth?

Solomon wouldn't argue against the benefits of wealth. What he might want to contend with is just *how* content we can become with wealth, and how illusory the sense of security can be. Remember that Solomon is interested in what is lasting and permanent.

In Chapter 2:18, (see Ecclesiastes 2:17–23 in the endnotes)[22] Solomon says, as he looks for something that gives meaning and purpose and lasts, 'I hated all the things I had toiled for under the sun, because I must leave them to the one who comes after me'. You see this with major players in the business world. People like Rupert Murdoch seem to find it so hard to let go and leave it all to someone else. Those of you who remember

Lachlan Murdoch and James Packer's One Tel disaster might think Mr Murdoch has good reason for clinging on to the very end!

A summary of Chapter 2 would be 'we work hard but it's all left to someone else, our work is never done and causes us stress and worry. Later he takes up a similar theme where he again argues for the meaninglessness of living life for possessions and money.

> Whoever loves money never has money enough
> Whoever loves wealth is never satisfied with
> his income. This too is meaningless
> (Ecclesiastes 5:10).[23]

Alain de Botton, a Swiss writer who now lives in London, wrote a brilliant book called *Status Anxiety*. He is very insightful about our society. What he essentially showed me about money and wealth, is that you can only eat one meal at a time, you can only sleep in one bed at a time, you can only drive one car at a time, but the minute money is linked to status, respect, the way you are seen by others and the way you see yourself, there can never be enough. That's why Mr. Murdoch and others find it so hard to retire or let go, because it's all linked to who we are. So then one billion isn't as good as two or three or four. It's never enough.

Ross Gittins, the Economics Editor for the *Sydney Morning Herald*, often writes about how little impact wealth has on our overall sense of wellbeing. Yet, he says, despite this evidence, studies show that Australians still believe just a little more money will make them happier.

As Solomon wraps up Chapter Five, he says very similar things to what he said in Chapter Two:

> I realised that it is good and proper for a man to
> eat and drink, and to find satisfaction in his
> toilsome labour under the sun during the few days
> of life that God has given him (Ecclesiastes 5:18).

If this is all there is, at least enjoy it the best you can; eat and drink and enjoy your work. It's all a vapour, a mist, but hey, make the most of it. The way to enjoy your life is to just accept a shallow hedonism, not to think too much and you can kind of get by.

'Under the sun', I wonder if the promise of money is a kind of a half-truth, it's a bit like Pethidene. If you have ever been in great pain, and been given Pethidene, you will know how good it is. I had a knee operation once, and I won't bore you with the details, but a lot of pain came with it and then I was given Pethidene and then ohhhh ... just fantastic stuff. It didn't fix the problem, but temporarily it made the pain go away.

'Under the sun', the best you can do is not to think too much and try and enjoy life. The problem is that many of us are finding that we are no longer satisfied with superficialities and materialism, and the people I know want to think about what life is all about. By midlife many of us are doing just that, and here's the thing—God *has* spoken to us and Solomon knows this. There is more to life than what we can see under the sun, and it is this perspective that Solomon is leading us towards.

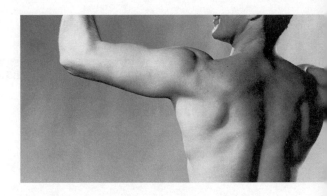

Chapter 10

Sex, pornography and withdrawal

'On a distant horizon she wanders my way,
So much to give and so little to say,
She's a creature of silence,
She's my imaginary girl.'

Hunters and Collectors 'Imaginary Girl', *Cut*, 1992

I am going to divert from Solomon and Ecclesiastes for a moment as we continue to consider different reactions of men to midlife.

Adultery

If you're looking for a quick fix, something that apparently offers excitement; the feeling of being appreciated, and powerful; that you've 'still got it', then an affair is likely. It's no real surprise that many men turn to adultery in midlife. After all, none of us has the harem that Solomon had to choose from.

Adultery is the great lie, but you can see what a powerful lie it is, and in midlife men are especially susceptible. It's not just the sex, it seems to offer all those things we long for—that feeling of being attractive, or finding someone who desires us, or feeling like a man. It's the thrill of the chase; of something new, and being reintroduced to real sexual passion. In the end what it delivers is pain, and hurts that never fully recover—bruises that won't heal and collateral damage.

The seduction of adultery starts long before sex. Most men do not plan to commit adultery. It happens at the end of a thousand little compromises. There are so many opportunities to put the brakes on, but if we don't we can find ourselves rolling down hill, with the whole thing gathering momentum and becoming harder to pull up. Along the way there are glances, and flirtatious remarks; lingering at work drinks parties and growing intimacy that we know goes beyond what our wives would be happy with.[24]

The collateral damage associated with adultery is profound. Rarely will a husband and father be thinking of his family as he checks into a hotel with another woman. Yet, he should know that his infidelity could lead his daughter or son to have major issues with trust and anxiety in the future, not to mention the profound sense of betrayal that a partner feels when the bond of exclusive love is broken. Hollywood might make adulterous sex look exhilarating, but the fallout from these relationships is rarely touched upon in the movies. Let's not kid ourselves. The road to adultery might be enticing but the cost is great and it is ultimately an act that diminishes us, and damages those we love.[25]

Pornography

Sometimes when the real world isn't too flash it is easier to deal with a make-believe one. That's the power of pornography. She's beautiful and available and smiles at me, and shows me her 'secrets'. So pornography becomes a bigger and bigger industry every year. It is becoming more mainstream and acceptable to the community. Gone are the days of brown paper bags and sleazy shops. The Internet has brought pornography into respectable lounge rooms. The 2003 *Australian Sexual Health and Relationship Survey* said 37% of men and 16% of women had looked at an x-rated movie in the last year, and Internet access will no doubt have increased such statistics since then. All of this gives weight to David Amsden's words that 'Cyber-porn has become the raunchy wallpaper to respectable lives.' While the stats below come out of the US, there is no reason to think Australia and other Western nations are significantly different.

- By the end of 2004, there were 420 million pages of pornography on the web.[27]

- The largest group of viewers of Internet porn is children between the ages of twelve and seventeen.[28]

- The Internet pornography industry generates US $12 billion dollars in annual revenue—larger than the combined annual revenues of ABC, NBC, and CBS.[29]

- 51% of pastors say Internet pornography is a possible temptation. 37% say it is a current struggle. Four in ten pastors have visited a porn website.[30]

- Pornography is physically more addictive than cocaine and 'imprints' the mind with images that are difficult if not impossible to erase. Overcoming pornography addiction takes years, and may affect you and everyone around you, for the rest of your life.

- The average age of first exposure to Internet porn is eight.[31]

- A study by Focus on The Family (March 2000) shows one in five adults in the US, 20%, (which is nearly 40 million people) have visited a sexually oriented web site.[32]

The addictive nature of pornography means that the amount and degree of the material needs to increase to achieve the same thrills. It alters the way men see women. Naomi Wolf, writing about the deleterious effects of pornography on the lives of both men and women writes,

> After all, pornography works in the most basic
> of ways on the brain: it is Pavlovian. An orgasm
> is one of the biggest reinforcers imaginable.
> If you associate orgasm with your wife, a kiss,
> a scent, a body, that is what, over time, will
> turn you on; if you open your focus to an
> endless stream of ever-more-transgressive
> images of cybersex slaves, that is what it will
> take to turn you on. The ubiquity of sexual
> images does not free eros but dilutes it.[33]

It changes the way we see our wives, and like junk food, for a moment it hits the spot, but after we have consumed it, we feel like rubbish and we know it's no good for us.

Pornography doesn't really deliver what it offers and, at best, leaves us feeling empty and at worst, profoundly damaged. It offers excitement, intimacy and power, but delivers none of this. The further this draws us into private voyeurism, hiding in the darkness, with fantasies that will never happen, the more it leaves us with a dead feeling that we are losers. She might be beautiful, and available, smiling at you, and showing you her secrets. But when you really think about it, if she met you in person, she wouldn't give a rat's about you, let alone show you anything. What is more, she's someone's daughter, and not the person you promised to love and cherish above all others.

So, rather than excitement and real engagement with a woman, where do we end up—hunched over in front of a computer screen? It's hardly a position of power or dignity.

Withdrawal

Other men, when faced with the pain and struggle of midlife will withdraw emotionally and mentally. They might be around physically but really their heart and soul has gone.

For some in this position the temptation will be to climb into a bottle, and find solace in drinking. This is not the heady partying of their younger days, but really a lonely escape from boredom and sorrow.

A mate of mine has been sober for six or seven years now, but before that drank often and hard. He helped me understand why some middle-aged men drink so much. He had just come back from his sister's funeral in another city. She was only in her 30s and died unexpectedly. He had just had a few days of visiting his family, going to the funeral, attending the wake and all the things that surround an event like that. 'It was really hard,' he told me, 'being sober all the time, I couldn't hide in the grog. When you get on the grog it all goes away. But when you're sober you have to face it.'

So some of the wrong reactions to the bricks of the midlife wall are adultery, or pornography, or withdrawal, or alcohol which are all ways of trying to cope, or more likely escape the midlife mire. Given all this most men simply ignore it and get on as best they can. They keep going to work, hang in there in their marriages, and as fathers, and in the occasional quiet moment when they stop, realise they are living a life of 'quiet desperation'.

Chapter 11

A frustrated universe

The whole range of human miseries, from restlessness and estrangement through shame and guilt to the agonies of daytime television— all of them tell us that things in human life are not as they ought to be.

Cornelius Plantinga, Jr.[34]

In the late 1980s the Scottish band Del Amitri put out a song called 'Nothing Ever Happens'. I'm writing for middle-aged men, so I feel comfortable bringing up a song from the dark ages. Some of you might remember it. The lyrics went like this:

Post office clerks put up signs saying position closed
And secretaries turn off typewriters
and put on their coats
Janitors padlock the gates
for security guards to patrol
And bachelors phone up their friends for a drink
While the married ones turn on a chat show
And they'll all be lonely tonight

and lonely tomorrow
Gentlemen time please,
you know we can't serve anymore
Now the traffic lights change to stop,
when there's nothing to go
And by five o'clock everything's dead
And every third car is a cab
And ignorant people sleep in their beds
Like the doped white mice in the college lab
Nothing ever happens, nothing happens at all
The needle returns to the start of the song
And we all sing along like before
And we'll all be lonely tonight and lonely tomorrow

Nothing Ever Happens — *Waking Hours*, Del Amitri (1989)

It's a great song, and easy to sing along with until you start really listening to the words and sometimes start to think, 'yeah it *is* like that, nothing ever happens'.

In Section 2 we have been speaking of Solomon's estimation of things and his fruitless search for satisfaction in pleasure, and possessions; in money and projects. In Chapter 1 of Ecclesiastes he also laments the fact that things pretty much stay the same—a common complaint of middle-aged men in Groundhog Day.

> What has been will be again, what has been
> done has been done again; there is nothing new
> under the sun. Is there anything of which one
> can say, 'Look! This is something new'? It was
> here already, long ago; it was here before our
> time (Ecclesiastes 1:9–10).

You might want to protest and say 'No, some things are new. What about technology?' In a sense you might be right.

Solomon couldn't email or use a mobile phone. But, I think the march of technology in another sense is not new. From the wheel to the space shuttle it's just people being inventive and clever, and humans have shown themselves capable of remarkable achievements. What is not new is that all of that technology and all that progress do not solve our problems. Half the planet goes to bed hungry at night while the other half struggles with obesity. The world is full of greed and selfishness and violence and nothing has changed. There is nothing new and technology will not fix it, no matter how much we dream.

So there it is—'under the sun', the world goes on forever, in an endless routine.

We are only here for five minutes, and even that can become boring and tedious and nothing ever changes and no one will remember us.

So, why is it that that doesn't seem right? Why does it feel like it shouldn't be this way? And why is it that all through human history, as far as I'm aware, every society has looked for something to give meaning and purpose and reasons for living? I think it's because we are wired up this way. Our world is not supposed to be this way and deep down we know it. In another part of the Bible the Apostle Paul writes to the followers of Jesus who lived in Rome. Look at what he says about our world:

> For the creation was subjected to frustration, not by its own choice, but by the will of the one who subjected it (i.e. God) (Romans 8:20).[35]

God has put frustration on our world. That word frustration is the same word that's used for meaningless in Ecclesiastes. It's that feeling that things are not right. And this frustration comes as early in the Bible as Genesis 3, where humanity walks away from God and God puts his heavy hand on humanity, in an attempt to have us walk back to him. Frustration and meaninglessness stem from this fracture in our relationship with God.

You may be sitting there thinking, 'Well there must be something that gives life meaning and purpose 'under the sun'—something that's not just a vapour'.

Solomon talks about some things that are fun; some things that are really good in life. He warns us though not to be fooled into thinking they are lasting or meaningful. The test he uses is: what has permanence, what lasts, what is not just a vapour?—I think its good for us to ask the questions too. It's good for me to stop and ask 'Am I living for something that in the end will be found to have been worthless or meaningless?'

Is there something that gives life meaning and purpose and satisfaction, something that will really last? The answer I think is a very big 'YES'! But it involves a Copernican revolution[36] in the way we see everything. We really do have to change the way we see the world and our place in it. It requires us to take God seriously, maybe for the first time.

A radical solution

Chapter 12

Eternity in our hearts

The life of a man is a long march through the night... One by one as they march, our comrades vanish from our sight, seized by the silent orders of omnipotent death.

Bertrand Russell[37]

Getting the seasons right

One of the most memorable passages of Ecclesiastes comes from Chapter 3 and it looks at the idea of time and how to understand it. On Solomon's journey in the search for meaning and purpose, we have seen him in the last few chapters look at pleasure, work, possessions and money and all those things have been seen to be good, but ultimately, 'under the sun', insubstantial and not of lasting significance.

Now his attention turns to the idea of time, and how to understand the seasons of our life. He gives us a poem here that is well-known—in fact it was the inspiration for a 1960s song that you might know, *Turn, Turn, Turn* by the Byrds. With a poem you have to read it and feel it, so let me quote the Ecclesiastes passage here in full:

There is a time for everything,
and a season for every activity under heaven:
a time to be born and a time to die,
a time to plant and a time to uproot,
a time to kill and a time to heal,
a time to tear down and a time to build,
a time to weep and a time to laugh,
a time to mourn and a time to dance,
a time to scatter stones and a time to gather them,
a time to embrace and a time to refrain,
a time to search and a time to give up.
a time to keep and a time to throw away,
a time to tear and a time to mend.
a time to be silent and a time to speak,
a time to love and a time to hate.
a time for war and a time for peace.
(Ecclesiastes 3:1–8).

Do you get the gist? It's the feeling of the pendulum, backwards and forwards, or perhaps the metronome, backwards and forwards, backwards and forwards. And what Solomon is saying is that life isn't just an endless flow of disconnected minutes; life is about seasons, the ebb and flow of seasons. Things come, things go.

He lists fourteen pairs of events that provide a picture of the whole of life. So there are the biggest events in life, our birth and our death, and smaller events like a time to sow and a time mend. You have the personal—love and hate; and the international—peace and war. What the writer wants us to see is that wisdom does not so much lie in a particular action, but in the timing. Wisdom lies much more in understanding the time or the season. Is it now the time to buy, or the time to sell? On the stock exchange, for instance, anyone can buy and sell, that's not hard, but knowing the timing, *when* to buy and sell, when to wait, makes all the difference in the world.

So what is one of the secrets to life? Solomon is saying it is understanding the season and being prepared for it. So if you understand the season and what is happening then you can, in a sense, work with the grain rather than against it. It's learning to understand the right event at the right time. In verse 11, he says 'He has made everything beautiful in its time'. The right event at the right time is beautiful. It might be the first cup of coffee in the morning or it might be the smell of spring, or it may be a hug from one of your kids. It could be finally getting the whole family around the table together at the right time. It is beautiful. Or it might be closing the deal over a long negotiation, and finally getting it nailed. Or it might be seeing roses grow after you have put so much time into them. Whatever it is that we are into, most of us have a sense of *the right thing at the right time*.

The opposite—when we get the timing all wrong; when the season is out of synch, can be tragic. A two year old stamping his feet can look kind of cute—at least to his parents, but the same petulance in an adult, is embarrassing. Perhaps that's why the stereotypical midlife crisis is such a joke.

I was picking up some take-away pizza recently and while I was waiting for it to come out of the oven, I noticed a middle-aged couple in the shop. They were obviously not long-time partners. They were being playful and flirty—she was in bare feet and he was cracking really bad jokes that everyone else could hear. Teenagers staffed the shop, and they were looking at these two with contempt, refusing to laugh at the man's jokes and clearly unimpressed. The irony was, the teenagers were acting like mature adults and the older couple were behaving like they were in high school, and they were making fools of themselves. Timing and seasons count. If you can remember being in a nightclub when you were young, and seeing an old person there, you will know what I mean.

But here is another thing—the poem tells us that ultimately we don't control our lives. The seasons of life wash over us, and the best we can do is fit in. It doesn't matter whether you have a palm pilot or wall planner, you won't have written in a time to mourn a year or two in advance. We don't ever write such a thing in our diary, but it comes. We don't plan the bad times or the sad times but they come, washing over us; we want to hold on to the good times and yet we cannot, because we don't ultimately control our lives. In fact the two biggest events, our birth and our death are completely beyond our control. The pendulum swings and the waves wash over us and we are powerless to stop it.

Eternity in our hearts

So, in view of all of that, in Chapter 3:9 Solomon asks the same question as he asked right at the beginning, 'What does the worker gain from his toil?' He goes on to say that given the way life is, given the pendulum swing, there is a vital issue that impacts every person's life.

> I have seen a burden that God has laid on men,
> he has made everything beautiful in its time.
> He has also set eternity in the hearts of men,
> yet they cannot fathom what God has done,
> from beginning to end (Ecclesiastes 3:10–11).

What's the burden God has placed on people? He has put *eternity* in their hearts, in our hearts. Now that's almost universally true, isn't it? Almost everyone believes there is something more to this life than just what they can see. Even if it's vague, for most people, there's a belief in the spiritual or supernatural; that there's something more than just the material.

Paul Davies is a physics professor at Macquarie University in Sydney. He wrote a very famous book called, 'The Mind of God'. Professor Davies isn't a Christian. But listen to what he says at the end of his book, as he looks at the physics of the universe:

> I cannot believe that our existence in this
> universe is a mere quirk of fate, an accident
> of history, an incidental blimp in the great
> cosmic drama. Our involvement is too intimate.
> The physical species homo may count for
> nothing, but the existence of mind in some
> organism on some planet in the universe is
> surely a fact of fundamental significance.
> Through conscious beings the universe has
> generated self-awareness. This can be no trivial
> detail, no minor by-product of mindless,
> purposeless forces, we are truly meant to be
> here.[38]

Eternity in his heart! I think he can see that and yet what does Solomon say in verse 11? 'Yet they cannot fathom what God has done from beginning to end.' We cannot work it out on our own. We need God's help.

One of my best mates ever was Arnie, a Rhodesian Ridgeback. At the end of his life he was pretty old, about thirteen years, and was beginning to fade, with arthritis and going a bit senile. In his prime he was a mighty dog—forty kilos of dynamite, a great watchdog. We ran miles and miles together. I remember eventually I said to the kids, 'I am going to have to take Arnie to the vet and get him put down'. They said, 'Dad, this is the third time you have told us this in a week'. 'Yeah, I am just trying to get you used to the idea', I replied. They said, 'No you're not, you're trying to get yourself used to the idea'. So anyway, I took him down to the vet and I held his head and patted him while he got the big green needle, and that was it. The dog gets old, and dies and he's buried.

Some time in the next forty years, maybe sooner, maybe later, I will die too. Maybe they will hold my hand while I go, and I'll be buried. And what will the difference be? Here is the human dilemma, folks, and I hope you can feel it too, and that is, *we live with eternity in our hearts and we die like our pets*. Eternity in our hearts, and we die like dogs.

> I also thought, "As for men, God tests them so
> that they may see that they are like the
> animals. Man's fate is like that of the animals;
> the same fate awaits them both: As one dies, so
> dies the other. All have the same breath; man
> has no advantage over the animal. Everything is
> meaningless. All go to the same place; all come
> from dust, and to dust all return
> (Ecclesiastes 3:18–20).

In verse 22 of Chapter 3, Solomon says, at least let's try to make the most of it, 'under the sun'.

> So I saw there is nothing better for a man than
> to enjoy his work, because this is his lot. For
> who can bring him to see what will happen after
> him?

'Under the sun', who knows what will happen after we die. We build, we demolish, we laugh, we weep, we're born, we die, and at least try to enjoy it while we are here, but don't think too much, 'under the sun'.

The problem is, many people I know do want to think. They might put it off for a while, but eventually people want to know where they will find meaning and purpose outside of themselves. When we get to that point the Bible speaks loudest to us.

Chapter 13

The punchline that changes everything

Every life is built fundamentally and finally on one's view of God.

Ravi Zacharias[39]

In this chapter, I want to explore why the book of Ecclesiastes is an antidote to the challenges and struggles of midlife. The argument of the ancient writer essentially states that 'under the sun', everything is meaningless (1:2 and 12:8). 'Under the sun', that is, without a word from God, the best we can do is to try to enjoy life with a kind of shallow hedonism; to not think too much because if we do, we will find before too long we will become disillusioned, and realise we are merely chasing after the wind.

But here's the good news. Right at the end of the book we get an Epilogue, just a few verses that change everything. They turn everything upside down, or perhaps I should say, right side up. They offer meaning and purpose.

At the end of Ecclesiastes we get an answer that relates to the reason we were created. I suggest that it's the fact that we *are* created that gives us purpose. If we are just the result of random, meaningless forces that just happen to evolve from matter, is it any wonder we might struggle to find meaning? No, the reason we ache for meaning is that we were created for something. So here it is, the punch line for the book of Ecclesiastes—a drum roll at this point would be appropriate! Solomon says:

> Now all has been heard; here is the conclusion of the matter. Fear God and keep his commandments, for this is the whole duty of man (Ecclesiastes 12:13).

That's it! That is the reason we can even hope for meaning and purpose. We are no longer 'under the sun'. This is not a closed universe. He is saying God *has* spoken to us, God *has* revealed himself. The frustration of meaninglessness is overcome not by a search through the things that humanity can offer, but only because 'under the sun' is a category that we need no longer apply.

So, in response to this the first thing he says is 'Fear God'. When you understand how great God is and how powerful God is, and pure God is, and how God hates wrong and evil, the proper reaction is to fear him. It's a word that carries the sense, not so much of terror (although that would not be entirely inappropriate), but rather a deep, reverent respect that acknowledges who God is, and who we are before him. Even within Christian circles today, I think we are a little light on this. We have turned God from the one we fear, to the one we'd like to have coffee with.

'Fear God', says Solomon and, 'Keep his commandments'. This is the first time in the whole twelve chapters of Ecclesiastes that Solomon has actually said that 'God has spoken to us'. As he writes here about 1,000 BC, his understanding is that God has spoken to Israel, in what we know as the Old Testament. God spoke to Abraham, Isaac, and Jacob. God spoke to his people particularly through the great prophet Moses, and then through other prophets. God spoke to them at Mount Sinai, gave them the Ten Commandments, and through the law, God told them how they should fear him and how they should respond to him.

The beautiful duty

How do we honour God? We live in obedience to him, says Ecclesiastes, and that is the whole reason we were made. We exist, to fear God and to keep his commandments. The great irony of this is, it's as we are obedient that we find freedom. As we live for him we will find our true purpose.

The voice inside us that says, 'But I want to make up my own mind, who is he to tell me how to live? I know better', is what the Bible calls 'sin'. It's walking away from God; it's saying to God, 'I'll run my life, not you'. And it shows itself in many different ways. The irony is that freedom, life, and purpose are found in obeying God and fearing him. It cuts against our natures so we need to hear it again and again - perfect freedom is found in service of him, as the old prayer book puts it. At the conclusion to his classic explanation of the Christian faith in *Mere Christianity*, C S Lewis says this about what it means to make Jesus the Lord of your life:

> Give yourself up, and you will find your real self.
> Lose your life and you will save it. Submit to
> death, death of your ambitions and favorite
> wishes every day ... submit with every fibre of
> your being, and you will find eternal life ... Look
> for yourself and you will find in the long run only
> hatred, loneliness, despair, rage, ruin and decay.

But look for Christ and you will find him, and
with him everything else thrown in![40]

This is what Lewis found to be the key to life after many
years of being an atheist.

Good news?

Solomon goes on in the last verse of the book to say why
our lives matter. Ecclesiastes says that life is examinable.

For God will bring every deed into judgment,
including every hidden thing, whether it is good
or evil (Ecclesiastes 12:14).

From cover to cover the Bible talks about the fact that
God will judge us. God will judge us by our actions, but also
by our motives. God knows our hearts. There will be a day
of reckoning, and the Bible talks a lot about heaven and hell.
They're relational terms; heaven is about knowing God and
living with him; hell is about being without God and existing
without him. The Bible is very clear that they are the two
great alternatives for eternity.

Is it good news? Well, its good news because all of a
sudden life has meaning and purpose; life matters. The
concept of God's judgment tells us that history—all of history,
including our own lives—is moving towards a goal. As New
Testament scholar Leon Morris put it, 'Judgment protects
the idea of the triumph of God and of good. Judgment means
that evil will be disposed of authoritatively, decisively,
finally'.

Here's a book that makes sense of our world and all that
has occurred in time and space and human history; and why
we feel that turmoil within us.

Solomon has shown us that our world is a mess. We live under this kind of futility and frustration. Things are wrong in our hearts, wrong in the way we treat each other, and in the way others treat us. The big picture of the Bible is that God will fix that; that God will deal with the frustration and futility and suffering, but only after he has dealt with evil completely.

Chapter 14
The biggest life

All the armies that have ever marched
All the navies that have ever sailed
All the parliaments that have ever sat
All the kings that ever reigned put together
Have not affected the life of mankind on earth
As powerfully as that one solitary life

James Allan, 1926

Stepping out of Ecclesiastes into the New Testament, the Apostle Paul as he writes to the Christians in the town of Corinth in the middle of the first century says essentially the same thing as Solomon, 'If this is all there is, if there is only life under the sun', (he doesn't use those exact words, but it is what he means), if this is all there is, well, 'Let us eat and drink for tomorrow we die'.[41] But the New Testament and the Apostle Paul argue that we don't have to live that way—because there is an event, something anchored in history, something we can know about, something we can be sure of that changes all of this—God has spoken to us. In fact God himself has turned up to give us something from 'beyond the sun' in the birth, life, death and resurrection of Jesus.

I put it to you that the solution to midlife dramas is not a philosophy, or a self-help programme, or buying a sports car, or getting fit, laid or rich. Meaning and purpose in life is found in following Jesus.

Here are some of the reasons why I am fired up about following Jesus as my King, even (and especially) as I become a middle-aged man:

His courage

As I read the gospel stories of Jesus' life, I'm struck by his courage. He keeps on speaking out against the religious leaders of the day, even when he knows the conspiracies to kill him are being hatched. In public debate, often with his life on the line if he slipped up and gave a wrong answer, his return of serve is brilliant.

We'll see in a later section that Jesus deliberately decides his time has come, and so walks the whole length of Israel on his way to Jerusalem knowing that every step takes him closer to being crucified. Most of us would like to think we could face death in a moment of crisis. In the heat of the moment we might sacrifice ourselves for someone we loved. But Jesus knows years in advance that he will do this, and deliberately walks towards it. That takes courage that I can hardly imagine.

The way he teaches

Nobody teaches the way Jesus does. The clarity and power of his stories are like being hit on the head with a wet newspaper. It's great that Jesus is so politically incorrect. He diagnoses the problem with our world, and says it is—us. He says the problem with us is pretty simple—we are evil—not the insipid nonsense that says we make 'unfortunate life choices', or that we're not acting 'to be all we can be'. Jesus says the problem is inside us, in our hearts:

> What comes out of a man is what makes him 'unclean'. For from within, out of men's hearts, come evil thoughts, sexual immorality, theft, murder, adultery, greed, malice, deceit, lewdness, envy, slander, arrogance and folly. All these evils come from inside and make a man 'unclean' (Mark 7:20–23).

Tell me that this list doesn't read like the pages of today's newspaper. It's not that we are as bad as we could be (we're not all Ted Bundy—with body parts in the freezer) but every part of our nature and character has been damaged by sin. And my heart, my desires, my motives are damaged. I've either done or wanted to do most of the list above, and if I haven't it's mostly through a matter of lack of opportunity or fear of the consequences.

What he teaches

I've talked a lot at the beginning of the book about life being damaged in so many areas and ways, and that we begin to see this more clearly as we get to midlife. It's not just that things are damaged but that it feels like it shouldn't be this way. When the Bible talks about redeeming the mess we have created, the focus turns to what it describes as 'the kingdom of God'. The thing that Jesus was most on about was this kingdom, and that it had arrived in him.

This kingdom is both present and future, in that it becomes a living reality in Jesus but won't fully arrive until after the final judgement. This 'kingdom' means that in

Jesus, God breaks into our world to establish himself as its true King. The kingdom of God is about God reversing the consequences of sin, both for individuals and for our world. At the beginning of Mark's gospel we learn that Jesus came proclaiming the good news of God.

"The time has come," he said. "The kingdom of God is near. Repent and believe the good news" (Mark 1:15).

The 'kingdom' is about God's promise to renew creation, where there will be no more mourning or crying or pain or death; a new creation where people will not grow old and die, and where God, not selfishness, will reign; where there will be no more sickness, loneliness and wasted lives. Jesus' message is that if we will have him as our King, we can be a part of this both now, and in eternity.

The way he treats people

In the early '90s I was the chaplain for the Sydney City Roosters Rugby League team. It's a funny thing to be a chaplain. You're the bottom of the social pecking order in the club,[42] and they're not really sure what to do with you. The thing I noticed was, it was the big men in the club who took the trouble to speak to the little baldy-headed chaplain. The one who impressed me most was Jack Gibson (then team manager). He had been a boyhood hero of mine, and general all-round Rugby League legend. When I finally met him I wasn't disappointed. He talked to me, was generous to me, even with his time, the most precious thing of all. I learned that the bigger the man the more time he has for little people.

That's what impresses me about Jesus. He had time for the little people. He had time for the important and the unimportant. He put the acid on the rich and powerful to follow him and wouldn't compromise. Jesus didn't care what other people thought of him, and he didn't play the social class game. He spoke to rich and poor the same way. Time after time he stopped a river of people who were following him to care for the weak—sometimes beggars, sometimes sick women, the social outcasts, prostitutes or tax collectors. He showed compassion for the poor, the weak, the nobodies. This is real compassion, the TV cameras weren't there to capture him kissing babies or helping beggars for the nightly news. Those who came to him honestly, looking for forgiveness, were always accepted and welcomed no matter what they had done.

His passion

The thing Jesus cared about more than anything else was treating God the right way. When Jesus arrived at the temple in Jerusalem and saw it used as a market place, he was furious. They were selling animals for sacrifice in the temple courts at inflated prices—ripping people off in the name of God—turning the worship of God into a greedy fiasco. John's gospel tells us what he did:

> So he made a whip out of cords, and drove all
> from the temple area, both sheep and cattle; he
> scattered the coins of the money changers and
> overturned their tables. To those who sold doves
> he said, "Get these out of here! How dare you
> turn my Father's house into a market!"
> (John 2:15–16).

Jesus cleared the whole market place. The temple courts were the size of a few football fields, with thousands of people, stalls, money, animals, and Jesus drove them out with a whip. There would have been a few welts handed out that day! All of that stemmed from Jesus' passion about giving due glory to God.

His sacrifice

Jesus came as God's promised King or Messiah, but the nature of his rule was anything but what the people expected or even hoped for.

> For even the Son of Man[43] did not come to be served, but to serve, and to give his life as a ransom for many (Mark 10:45).

He came to serve. His whole life was about serving others. Sometimes his life was so crowded that he didn't even have time to eat. At one stage he was so tired he fell asleep on a boat in a storm. He had time for people, and compassion for the crowds.

But of course his greatest sacrifice was to die on the cross, as he says, to give his life as a ransom for many. There are many admirable things about Jesus' life and lots of people who are not Christians will gladly speak of those. But it is at the cross and then at his resurrection that we really see the uniqueness of Jesus. The message of the cross of Jesus is, that he went willingly to his death at the hands of injustice, corruption, and hatred so that the wrath of God's judgement will not fall on you and me. He died in our place, so we can be forgiven. This remains the greatest act of true love ever.

The resurrection
(and what it tells us about who he is)

In Jesus we have someone who has overcome the power of death. What was lost from the original creation will one day be completely restored because of what Jesus has done. So, our response to him is critical to living a life of meaning and hope. Nothing and no one else comes even close to being as significant as this fact. Many of us who have been followers of Jesus for many years, still, on occasion, need to be shaken out of complacency at this startling good news, which, if it is true, changes everything.

I want to live a big life like Jesus did. I want to urge you to live big as well. We cannot hope to be like Jesus in any complete way, but we can follow him, and trust him, and look to his example of what a life worth living might look like— a life of integrity, service, kindness, passion and sacrifice. A life lived in response to what Jesus has done.

Chapter 15

A revolution lived out

*True freedom is the freedom to be one's
true self, as God made us and meant us to be.*

John Stott[44]

What difference does following Jesus make to midlife? It changes everything—or at least it *should* change everything.

We are not just unimportant, pathetic, selfish little creatures, eeking out meaningless lives, as we wait for a slow death and an inevitable end to our existence. Follow Jesus and you have someone to live for; someone and something bigger than just you. You can live big.

In our boring little lives in suburbia, in the struggle of our marriages, or in the heartache of divorce, as we sit in the endless lines of traffic, as we sit in a cubicle at work, as we lay our billionth brick or drive our billionth nail, or do endless unseen laps on dark nights in a tractor—as we sigh and shake our heads about teenage ingratitude—as we live through Groundhog Day—taking Jesus seriously and truly following him offers us the promise—not from me but from him—of a revolution in the way we see the world and our place in it. Everything changes, because he changes our hearts.

The potential for change is enormous—in the next three chapters I'll try to summarise three areas where this can be the case. Each one will set us free.

Revolution I

Midlife is just a beginning when eternity is in view

This world is not all there is. There is a much more important reality—eternity.

In Section I, I talked about the time in a man's life when he can finally begin to sense his own mortality. In many ways this is the beginning of wisdom. Seeing things from the perspective of eternity changes the way we'll respond to our impending death. Our lives are not half over, we are just at the beginning. We can seriously believe it, because Jesus promised it. My time here may be more than half over, but my time isn't going to run out.

When we follow Jesus we need not fear death. The New Testament says Jesus has taken the sting out of death. There will still be sorrow at separation from people we love and yet we will not grieve without hope. We will live our lives knowing that we will die, not with a sense of fear but with a sense of urgency that there is much important stuff to be done.

As your family and friends gather at your funeral what would you want them to say about you? (Assuming that they actually tell the truth rather than turn you into some stained glass saint). On your deathbed what do you want to be able to say about your life? Let me tell you some things that no one ever said on their death bed: 'I wish I had spent more time at work', 'I wish I had built a bigger house', 'I wish I had climbed higher on the corporate ladder', 'I wish I had watched more television', 'I wish I had spent more time watching sport'. What will matter when we draw our last breath is people, and what we have shared with them. Investing in people is also an investment in eternity. Work out how many years you have got left and start investing in what really matters—people. Even if you have done a very ordinary job in the first half of your life you can make a massive investment and a huge difference in the second half.

Read the gospels[45] and you see how clearly Jesus sees things from the perspective of eternity, how we forgive people, how we stand up to copping a hard time, the urgency of seeking God's kingdom, the foolishness of gaining the whole world and yet losing our souls. It's all seen from the viewpoint of eternity and how brief our lives are here.

I'm a bit thick but I'm finally beginning to get it. I've started counting life in a different way. Instead of thinking I'm in my late forties and all the good stuff is gone, I now think 'the best is yet to come—I better get on with it'. I'm now forty-eight, if God gives me until seventy-five, that's another twenty-seven years. Instead of moping around thinking 'Where are all my dreams? My life is half over', I am now thinking, (sometimes I need a reminder as well) it's twenty-seven years to eternity, I need to use this time the best I can. I'll have a long time to think back on what I did with these years. So, rather than thinking how can I indulge my middle-aged male selfishness (which still regularly rears its ugly bald head) I want to get on serving Jesus, trying to be a useful part of the community he has placed me in. I want other people to know him too, so a lot of my energy is dedicated to helping others understand the good news of Jesus.

An eternal perspective changes our priorities. It can help us to be less worried about the present, even while we are fully engaged with it. I think of it as being able to walk more lightly in our world. As Jesus said:

> Therefore I tell you, do not worry about your life, what you will eat or drink; or about your body, what you will wear. Is not life more important than food, and the body more important than clothes? Look at the birds of the air; they do not sow or reap or store away in barns, and yet your heavenly Father feeds them. Are you not much more valuable than they? Who of you by worrying can add a single hour to his life? And why do you worry about clothes? See how the lilies of the field grow. They do not labour or spin. Yet I tell you that not even Solomon in all his splendour was dressed like one of these. If that is how God clothes the grass of the field, which is here today and tomorrow is thrown into the fire, will he not much more clothe you, O you of little faith? So do not worry, saying, 'What shall we eat?' or 'What shall we drink?' or 'What shall we wear?' For the pagans run after all these things, and your heavenly Father knows that you need them. But seek first his kingdom and his righteousness, and all these things will be given to you as well. Therefore do not worry about tomorrow, for tomorrow will worry about itself. Each day has enough trouble of its own (Matthew 6:25–34).

This is what I call a worldview transformation if we follow it. I now have something bigger to worry about than my own little ambitions. My master tells me to seek first his kingdom. The kingdom of God as Jesus teaches is not a place or an institution. He is really speaking about establishing

God's reign, at present, in the hearts of his people. God's people know him and serve him as their king.

This change of focus or priorities is easy enough to say, but it takes the rest of a lifetime to put into practice. But as we do this, it will set us free—free from living for trivia, like what we eat, drink, or wear. We still need this stuff but we can know it's not the point of life.

Chapter 16

Revolution 2
Life is found in service not selfishness

I have come that they may have life, and have it to the full.

Jesus (John 10:10).

The second great worldview change in following Jesus is realising I am not the centre of the universe. Jesus is. It's simple really, but putting this one into practice isn't easy.

If Jesus is the centre of the universe, real life, real freedom is found in what I was made to do—to serve him. A lot of what fuels midlife problems is a selfish focus—a focus on me and what I want.

The problem with selfishness is where it leads; the end point is being alone. Those who live life and treat people as if it all revolves around them end up alone, or at least with an ever-decreasing circle of people who are prepared to care about them. It's the opposite of living big. Living selfish is living small.

The foundation for living for Jesus stems from the fact that he made us, He is the image of the invisible God, the firstborn over all creation.

> For by him all things were created: things in heaven and on earth, visible and invisible, whether thrones or powers or rulers or authorities; all things were created by him and for him. (Colossians 1:15-16).

We were made for him, he owns us. In fact he owns us in two ways; he created us, and he bought us. He paid a price for us, his life, and bought us back from the penalty of sin.

> Do you not know that your body is a temple of the Holy Spirit, who is in you, whom you have received from God? You are not your own; you were bought at a price. Therefore honour God with your body. (1 Corinthians 6:19-20).

So Jesus made us, and he bought us back at the price of crucifixion. In the Bible's language, we've been created and redeemed by Jesus. We belong to him, and our reason for existence is to serve him. As I said in Chapter 12, the beautiful irony of belonging to Jesus is, as we serve him we will find life.

I suppose many men think 'I don't want to serve anyone or anything, I want to be free'. But the reality is, that never happens—we always serve someone or something. It may be serving career, or our reputation or money, or our hormones, and behind all these things is serving the need for status or security.

In the end, serving anything or anyone other than Jesus is not freedom but slavery.

Jesus says 'follow me'. He was the greatest servant of all—the master who washed his disciples feet and who went around tired and hungry and poor—exhausted himself walking, preaching and healing others. And most of all he became a servant, to the point of death on the cross. So when Jesus says, follow me and be a servant he already has the runs on the board.

Real life, real satisfaction is found in following and serving Jesus because in doing this we will become more like Jesus—more like the people we were meant to be. It doesn't mean it will be easy. In fact you can guarantee it won't be. The easy things in life don't change us much. It is God's plan to make his men like Jesus.

The Spirit

Very importantly Jesus promises not to leave us alone in this, battling it out in our own strength. He promises the Holy Spirit to guide and empower us to live the life of the kingdom.

> And if the Spirit of him who raised Jesus from
> the dead is living in you, he who raised Christ
> from the dead will also give life to your mortal
> bodies through his Spirit, who lives in you
> (Romans 8:11).

Without the Spirit we wouldn't have much hope, but he is a crucial element of living the Christian life as we get serious about serving Jesus and being like him. We need to be open to the Spirit as we read God's word and pray to him—hanging out with Jesus, allowing him to work change in our hearts and in our lives.

Many people today preach a version of the Christian message that says, 'God wants you to realise your potential, he wants to make you healthy, wealthy, beautiful and successful and prosperous.' Like most good lies it's half true. God does want you to realise your potential, and turn you into someone special—he plans to make you like Jesus. The tough news is it's going to be hard work. Look at Jesus' life, and what he went through, and what it cost. The book of Hebrews says he 'learned obedience'—that he was made the perfect saviour through suffering.

As we set out to serve Jesus, the first thing he tells us is serve other people. So, husband, father, son, friend, work mate, employee, boss, it's about service. This is not the same as being a doormat. Service is the determination to act in the other person's best interest; to look out for the interests of others; to be thoughtful and actively engaged in making other people's lives better. And sometimes that may mean caring enough for them to be in conflict with them; to tell them what they need to hear rather than what they want to hear. Sometimes we may kick someone's butt because we love them. Service is costly, but this is the path to life; to living a life that will be bigger than just us, and our own small ambitions.

Chapter 17

Revolution 3
Faith in action—learn to be dependent, so you can learn to be independent

*When I am yours, then at last
I am completely myself.*

Michelangelo

The Christian life of following Jesus is about faith. Faith isn't some mystical feeling; it's really another way of saying trust. If we have faith in Jesus it means we trust him. And it is simply that trust in him that will save us:

> For it is by grace you have been saved, through faith—and this not from yourselves, it is the gift of God—not by works, so that no one can boast. For we are God's workmanship, created in Christ Jesus to do good works, which God prepared in advance for us to do (Ephesians 2:8–10).

Faith, trust or dependence will change us in many ways, but here are three ways that I could think of:

1) Gratitude and joy

We must realise that we don't have to try to win God's favour, earn enough credit points, or obey the rules well enough to earn his love and forgiveness. Understanding being saved by faith alone will transform 'religion' from rules, to living with gratitude and joy.

2) Independence

When we understand that we are dependent on God, and answerable only to him we live with an 'audience of one'. So much of men's lives are lived with concern about status, and how other people see them. Why do you think blokes care about wanting the corner office, or the show pony ute, or the trophy blonde girlfriend? It's all about what others will think of us. It affects how much we drink, or how hard we work, and what we dream about, plan for and strive to achieve.

When we move to having an audience of one it sets us free. It comes down to a question of where it is that we find our identity. Is it in the role we play as the hard worker, or the responsible provider, or the big partier, or the sporting great? Do we gain our sense of identity by the job we do, or the suburb we live in, the car we drive or the friends we have? Dependence on God means that we find our identity primarily in him.

Why do you think Jesus was so independent in the way he spoke to people? He could be honest and tough when needed, or compassionate and gentle, because he lived in dependence on God, and understood God was the only audience that mattered. He was unaffected by what other people thought of him. Learn this lesson and we can do what's right rather than just what's popular; we'll be able to treat other people the right way. Learn to live your life 'looking up' and not 'looking sideways', and it will change everything.

3) Trust versus worry

He is the boss and he'll look after us. Understand that God is in control, of everything, and that he plans to look after his people. In fact he plans to use everything in life to make them like Jesus. So what is there to worry about? The more we learn to live by faith—the more we should learn not to worry—to pray and leave things in God's hands and get on with serving him, knowing he has everything under control.

For most of us who hit middle-age, life has taken at least some toll on us. We have our scars; our 'what ifs' and 'if onlys'. And yet, when you understand God's promise in Romans 8:28 'and we know that in all things God works for the good of those who love him, who have been called according to his purpose,' we can understand even the hard things differently. God promises that in everything that happens to us he will work for our good.

What is our ultimate good? 'To be conformed to the likeness of his son' (Romans 8:29). The good news is God will make us like Jesus. The bad news is, this almost always involves pain; the good times in life rarely change us. It is the hard times that mould and shape our character, teaching us humility, compassion and empathy for other people.

Whatever disappointments, whatever heartaches that have happened in the first half of life, God is able to take them and use them for good. Does that mean that the heartaches and disappointments won't hurt? No, it means that in that pain we can be transformed, and grow more like Jesus. For some of us men it is only pain that will bring us to realise our need of finding God and finding forgiveness.

There are many other things about learning to live by faith or trust in God, but how about those three for a start:

i) joy and gratitude, not life-crushing rules

ii) freedom from looking sideways all the time

iii) freedom from worry about the future.

Chapter 18

The revolution on the ground
Marriage and family

The life I live in the body, I live by faith in the Son of God, who loved me and gave himself for me

(Galatians 2:20b).

That life is found in service, rather than selfishness, is nowhere more true than in marriage and family. We need to love our wives and families with eternity in view. Our greatest goal must be to help present them as mature followers of Jesus on the last day.

If I think my marriage exists to serve me, and of what I can get out of it, it won't work, or at least won't work very well. The problem with many marriages is that both partners are thinking 'What can I get out of it?' Like a tick on a dog—with both partners thinking that, we end up with two ticks and no dog.

If your marriage needs a defibrillator, here are some thoughts on how to get things jump-started.

Stand up and be a man—one of the great problems with marriage in our society is what might be called the 'husband as a lovable dope' syndrome. Men are portrayed as following their wives around, always in the wrong, not knowing what goes on, obeying orders, well meaning but generally incompetent and stupid. Men are the butt of jokes in view of the all-knowing, all-competent woman who is in control. This is an image that comes through from sitcoms and movies and especially television ads where frequently the husband is the idiot and the wife has all the answers.

And unfortunately it is so often true, in the sense that men take on this role—anything for a quiet life! So many men have given up and get led around by the nose, letting their wife wear the proverbial pants. Steve Biddulph can see the problem:

> The millions of men who adopt this stance
> find that it rarely, if ever, leads to happiness.
> Women with dopey husbands are not happy—
> they actually become more dissatisfied, more
> complaining. Often without even realising
> why, the hen-pecking behaviour escalates—
> for a simple reason. Deep down, women want
> to engage with someone as strong as them.
> They want to be debated with, not just agreed
> with. They hunger for men who can take the
> initiative sometimes, make some decisions, let
> them know when they are not making sense.
> It's no fun being the only adult in the house.
> How can a woman relax or feel safe when the
> man she is teamed with is so often soft and
> weak? I have counselled many strong,
> capable feminist women who tell me they
> have finally found the sensitive, caring, new
> age man they **thought** they wanted and they
> are **bored stiff**! They are starting to drive
> slowly past building sites, and wondering
> whether to whistle![46]

What he is saying is right. Your wife doesn't need you to be a puppy. Our Staffordshire terrier puppy says hello by lying on his back, four legs in the air showing his belly. I guess he is saying 'You are the boss. Do I get a belly scratch for being a good boy?' I feel like saying to him 'Mate sit up straight and act like a man!' Well a dog anyway. Have some self-respect. It is bad enough when a puppy does it, but when a husband does it, it is not cute at all, plus you get your shirt really dirty. I think most women want someone who will carry more than their share of the load. A wife wants to feel safe and loved and secure because she is married to a strong man whom she knows loves her and is reliable.

More than anything else the mark of being a man is the willingness to take responsibility. The Bible's prescription for marriage is very different to the way many in our society think. In Ephesians 5 the Apostle Paul outlines the way Christian marriages are to work:

> Wives, submit to your husbands as to the Lord.
> For the husband is the head of the wife as Christ
> is the head of the church, his body, of which he
> is the Saviour. Now as the church submits to
> Christ, so also wives should submit to their
> husbands in everything. Husbands, love your
> wives, just as Christ loved the church and gave
> himself up for her to make her holy, cleansing her
> by the washing with water through the word, and
> to present her to himself as a radiant church,
> without stain or wrinkle or any other blemish,
> but holy and blameless. In this same way,
> husbands ought to love their wives as their own
> bodies. He who loves his wife loves himself.
> After all, none ever hated his own body, but he
> feeds and cares for it, just as Christ does the

church—for we are members of his body. For this
reason a man will leave his father and mother
and be united to his wife, and the two will
become one flesh. This is a profound mystery—
but I am talking about Christ and the church.
However, each one of you also must love his wife
as he loves himself, and the wife must respect
her husband (Ephesians 5:20–33).

Notice that the husband is to be the head of the wife. Headship in the Bible doesn't mean being an authoritarian Nazi but it does mean having responsibility to lead and care for your wife. What does it look like in practice? 'Husbands love your wives as Christ loved the church and gave himself up for her' (verse 25). The way a husband is to love his wife is to give his life for her day by day and to act in her best interest and to care for and to love her. This is not being pushed around. It is also not the same as being a selfish mongrel and ignoring her and what she needs. A husband is to love her, take the initiative in caring for her, listen to her, spend time with her. The model for how to love your wife is the same way as Jesus loved his church and gave his life for her. It's about sacrifice and intentional, thoughtful, selfless love. Here's the thing. Life will be better if you practice this and you'll be pleasing not only your wife but Jesus as well.

One other thing to note is the Apostle Paul tells wives to submit to their husbands. Submission means a willing acceptance of his headship or leadership. She is to make it pleasant for him to lay his life down for her and to care for her; pleasant rather than difficult. But note, nowhere does Paul say a husband is to make his wife submit. A husband's job is to love her and to care for her, to lead her, to do what is best for her, but not to *make* her submit.

If she is not submissive it is not your job to make her submit. That is between her and God.

What will it look like to lay down your life for your wife? It probably won't mean taking one big bullet for her, but it may mean taking a hundred smaller decisions day-by-day. You lay down your life for her as you care for her, listen to her, help her with housework; as you go into bat for her with difficult teenagers or kids who don't show her proper respect. In fact just writing this makes me realise that I have a long way to go at home as well.

In his book *The Five Love Languages*, Gary Chapman outlines the different ways in which people, in this case our wives, are able to accept love. He says people look for love in different ways. The five that he outlines are:

1. Physical touch
2. Words of affirmation
3. Quality time
4. Gifts
5. Acts of service

He says each person has one or more of these, which are their love language; the way in which they look for love.[47]

My wife is not interested in money or presents or expensive dinners out. None of these compare with walking a dog together. For Kathy, her love language is time together. The best way that I can show Kathy I love her is to grab the dog and spend an hour walking and listening and talking with her. It is well worth the time to understand your wife's love language. I know the average bloke thinks his wife's love language is, or at least should be, physical touch (and that is important) but there will be other ways particularly that your wife is wired up to accept love. It may be spending time with her, it may be a little present now and then, it may take some experimenting but you will be smart enough to work it out. How does your wife want you to show you love her? Work it out and I guarantee you will be glad you did.

The revolution we need to learn with regard to sex is that life is found in service not in selfishness. Very many of men's complaints and frustrations about sex come from our selfishness rather than setting out to serve our wives. It doesn't mean that women are without fault but it does mean that men need to learn to take the initiative to serve and care for and love our wives rather than simply expect them to perform sexually for us. The irony is when we do learn to serve and love and to care for them our sex lives will improve out of sight.

We men need to learn to love and lead our families. Some men attempt to withdraw and be distant and disengage, other men want to rule the roost with an iron hand. The way to lead a family is by engaging, being there, knowing them and then taking the lead in caring for them. Sometimes this will mean stopping them doing what they want because it is no good for them.

For those who are divorced I want to acknowledge the pain of that, and say that despite the heartache the same principles of sacrificial love discussed here apply to other relationships with our kids, wider families, friends and communities. As in marriage, the rewards are great when we put others ahead of ourselves.

Chapter 19

Midlife (and beyond) worth living

I know this now. Every man gives his life to what he believes. Every woman gives her life for what she achieves. Sometimes people believe in little or nothing, so they give their lives to little or nothing ...

Joan of Arc[48]

So with the changed perspective of life no longer under the sun; living for Jesus as the true King, does Groundhog Day disappear? I suggest the answer to that question is both yes, and no.

Wild at Heart by John Eldredge has been one of the most popular Christian books for men (and women), in the last few years.[49] I want to be fair to John Eldridge as he makes some good points, and appeals to some real issues. He is writing to men's hearts. Eldridge is arguing that men and especially Christian men, have been domesticated, even emasculated (my words not his), and this domestication, removal of risk, and the general culture of tame niceness, has sucked the life out of us. This rings true for me, 'Please God don't let me be just "nice".'

He says that if we follow Jesus, life will become a great adventure. Eldredge's books argues every man wants:

- A battle to fight
- A beauty to rescue
- An adventure to live

This is his model for the Christian life. Follow Jesus and he will give us the adventure to live. 'Life is not a problem to be solved; it is an adventure to be lived', he says.

One of the key turning points in his life is when he picks up a book by Gil Bailey, which says:

> 'Don't ask yourself what the world needs. Ask yourself what makes you come alive, and go do that, because what the world needs is people who have come alive.'[50]

So he heads off to do what will make him come alive.

He may be right that this is what men want. But is it what Jesus promises? In *Wild at Heart,* Eldredge is working hard against the emasculation that comes with suburbia, and if I may say, especially Christian suburbia, and it is important to address this. But I can't help feeling that he's just baptised the American frontier dream, and made it that Jesus calls us to the great adventure.

It depends on what you mean by 'adventure'. I don't see the word adventure in the Gospels. Jesus does call us to take up our cross and follow him; to lay down our lives in the service of others.

The great irony is—and this is a key point of my book that I hope you haven't missed—it is in living that life of service that we will find life; true life that is rewarding, fulfilling and meaningful.

Real life is found not in self-service but in the service of Jesus and then others, and that life is truly heroic.

So taking up the advice of Gil Baily (and John Eldredge) above, I would want to adjust that to 'what the world needs is those who will lay down their lives in the service of others'.

I know I sound like a killjoy—I did say at the beginning of this book I was middle-aged and grumpy—but what I'm trying to hose down (and there are many that talk this way) is the promise of the great adventure; that life will be thrilling if you follow Jesus—you'll be successful, your potential will be unlocked and you will be on an ever-upward spiral to success in a worldly sense.

But what happens when a middle-aged punter who follows Jesus looks around and says. 'But my life still looks like going to work at a boring job, standing on the train with the other commuters staring at blank faces with the screen saver on. My marriage is still boring, my kids are still ungrateful little rats, church is ordinary and full of boring people like me. This doesn't feel like a great adventure.' Instead of fooling ourselves and saying 'Yes! this is great, just see the adventure we're in, commute number 199740 will be exciting today', how about we try being honest and saying—life is hard and sometimes very boring; there are things in our lives that are genuinely painful; and people who are hard work, and there are emotional scars that we carry that won't go away.

Ploughing our way through all this isn't an adventure, but (and this is a big but) it *does* have value in eternity. Did you get that? We must see our lives from the perspective of eternity. Some men will follow Jesus and it will mean a martyr's death in the Coliseum in the first century, or prison and beatings in the twenty-first century or winning thousands to Christ as great preachers. Others will follow him, and plug on through suburbia year after year, dying the death of 1000 commutes, because they choose to love and serve those Jesus has given them. And one day—when they appear before the great white throne—Jesus will say to them 'Well done good and faithful servant—you lived your life for me in suburbia, you loved your wife, and kids, you fed them, you cared for them, because that's what I asked, well done—just come and see what I have planned for you.'

Now that I have hosed this down and said that following Jesus means taking up your cross, let me say that in another sense, following Jesus *can be* a great adventure. We never know where he will take us in life, and he has big things for us to do. Sometimes it may be difficult, sometimes it may be boring but if we set out to truly follow Jesus, life will be far bigger than it ever would have been with our own small ambitions. We are being invited into the biggest life possible.

When we follow Jesus, he promises to walk with us, to never leave us and to show us how to truly live.

We can live big in suburbia, live a big life wherever we are, because we are living for something bigger than just ourselves.

Chapter 20

Surviving and thriving— why midlife can be beautiful

'What do I wish to be remembered for?'

I suggest that midlife is a time when, under God, we can make a difference and we can actually enjoy it.

In his book *Half Time*—Bob Buford, a very successful business man, speaks about the profound effect that the drowning death of his son Ross had on him. He realised his goals and priorities for the second half of his life needed to change.

> I used this physical prayer when I spoke at a church two and half weeks after we buried Ross: (with palms up) "God you have given my life into my hands. I give it back to you, my time, my property, my life itself... knowing it is only an instant compared to my life with you (and with Ross) in eternity."
>
> (With palms down) I concluded, "Father, to you, I release the cares and concerns of this world, know

you loved me enough to give your only Son on my behalf. I'm a sinner in need of a saviour and, once again I accept what you have done for me as sufficient, In Jesus' name. Amen."[51]

St Augustine said that asking yourself the question 'What do I wish to be remembered for?' is the beginning of adulthood.

If the first half of life is a great quest for success the second half is a journey to significance.[52] Don't allow the second half of your life to be characterised by decline, boredom, and increasing ineffectiveness for the kingdom.

Looking back—pain can be gain

In the first half of life there may well have been pain that could leave you bitter. It may be necessary to look it in the face, forgive those involved, and forgive yourself, and move on. See if you can see the positives that have come from it, even if the only positives have been the hard lessons you've learned.

Too many people approach the second half of their lives with regrets over the first half... (I should have spent more time with my family... I should have developed better relationships... I should have...) It haunts them in ways that sap the inspiration to go on to better things. So, one of the first things you need to do is make peace with your first-half set of issues. 'Half time' is not about beating yourself up for what you did not do, but for coming to terms with your failures and recognising that you live under grace.

As we begin or continue to construct lives of meaning and purpose in midlife and beyond, there are some important things we will do well to remember.

Have some fun

When we give our lives to follow Jesus we are acknowledging that God is in charge of us and of the world. And it is actually because we believe God is in charge that we can take some time off and have fun. God has made us to be able to enjoy the good world that he has given us with all sorts of great things from friends and family to good food, sport and entertainment—the list is almost endless. In middle-age we need to be deliberate about having some fun.

There is a need for balance and, as Ecclesiastes would say, a time for everything. When we understand the work of Jesus in making all of life meaningful, renewing the whole of a fallen creation, we can celebrate the wonder and beauty of the good things God has given us to enjoy. I once heard about an ex-surfer who had become a Buddhist monk. He had given up surfing because he came to see it as a meaningless pursuit. 'Under the sun' (pardon the pun) he was right I guess, but the perspective of the Bible is that even the meaningless becomes meaningful when we live our lives under God. We can enjoy God's good creation, knowing that it is also not the totality of life.

So what do you do to have fun? For me there are two different ways this works. I have some regular stuff I do that's fun and helps let off steam and I have my once-a-year trip away.

The regular fun is that I exercise about six days a week. Sometimes it's running and sometimes it's weights at the gym. It all happens before 7:00am. I do this to keep physically well, but I also do it so that I don't go crazy. My wife would love it if I liked board games, but the sight of a jigsaw puzzle can make me start to lose the will to live. I need to do the physical stuff to 'let off steam'. Not everyone shares my love of exercise, but for me—it's a tonic. The last few years I've trained for a half-marathon with a few mates. It helps keep me sane.

The other thing I do once a year is I go away for a week in the bush. I know it's not politically correct but I love hunting. I shoot feral pigs. I call it eco tourism—it *is* actually helping the environment.

I spend one week a year in the bush with my brother or one of my mates, shoot pigs and live like one, and it's great. It's like getting an enema from city life. I spend one week doing this and 51 planning it. I guess you could call it a hobby. I plan different trips to different places, put the gear together, organise food and so on. I daydream about being in Cape York, or western NSW. My point is simple really. We all have to cope with Groundhog Day, and when you become a Christian that doesn't disappear. So you need to have something in your life that is fun. It might be a sport, or a hobby. But you need to do something that recharges your batteries, and I don't mean the television. In small doses it can be OK, but television just deadens the brain.

Different blokes I know are learning golf, or doing self-defence, going to boxing classes, or ballroom dancing with their wives. Other men I know are doing a fancy cooking course. Others play touch footy, play an instrument, do an art class or learn a language. So work out what it is for you, get organised, ensuring that it doesn't destroy family life. The other day I heard of a bloke whose wife left him because of golf. He would work all week, and then spend all day Saturday at the golf course leaving his wife alone. After a while she had had enough. We all make our choices, but I reckon his golf buddies are not going to cuddle up beside him and feed him when he is old. Bad choice I'd say. So negotiate it with your wife and you can have a win/win.

Hopefully she'll realise the benefits from having a husband who has some fun occasionally, who lets steam out of the pressure cooker.

For some of us there is a need to head for the wide-open spaces. There are many books about the need to get out in the wilderness to get in touch with our wild roots. It depends on who you are. Some men just aren't into all this out door stuff, and it's not necessary to be a man. For some though, there is something very therapeutic about time in the bush. To sleep where you can see the stars, to hear magpies in the morning, to cook around the fire, and watch the 'bush television'[53] is for many blokes a cleansing experience. It may be that there's something special about the bush and nature, or it may be that the peace and quiet and slowing down is good for us.

There are guys that I know who organise golfing, fishing, or surfing trips with their friends. Wine tasting and art excursions are more to some people's liking. Whatever it is you are in to, find something that helps you to relax, have fun, and celebrate God's creation.

Invest in relationships

Men need to make the effort to keep long-term friends. By midlife it can be more difficult to make new friends and between family and work responsibilities it can be very difficult to find time for people. This makes it all the more important to keep old friendships strong. You have to be organised and proactive about this, or they will easily drop off the radar screen.

I have some mates with whom I have shared thirty years of friendship. I keep notes in my diary to make sure I see these guys regularly. Not every week, but every couple of months we get together. Blokes tend to need a reason to ring each other and generally do stuff together when they catch up. So get organised with your long-term mates, go to the football, go fishing, surfing or whatever it is you like doing together. It is hard to replace people who have known you for a long time and understand something of your history. It's too much to expect your wife and kids to be your only friends, or to meet all your needs.

Accumulated resources can help others

If things go well for you, money and resources accumulate as you get older. You may have access to houses and cars and maybe receive an inheritance somewhere along the line. Part of middle-age is the maturity to realise that you are just a steward of this wealth. It all belongs to God, we won't take it with us, and we'll be held accountable for what we have done with it. Now I know you need to be financially responsible and provide for your wife and kids, and for your retirement, but midlife often presents the opportunity for some serious generosity.

Care for the poor is a critical aspect of life for those who are followers of Jesus and have the means to offer help to those less fortunate. Love God and your neighbour is not a suggestion, it is a commandment (as Bono from U2 keeps reminding us). Many of us can afford to be looking for opportunities to help others out with places to stay when they are needed, cars to drive to get them out of a tricky situation, financial gifts to individuals and organisations. Healthy and regular financial contributions to the life of our local church can be seen as an opportunity to play a part in God bringing others to know him. Even being really generous in having people over for meals and making them feel welcome in our homes can be a good way to respond to God's kindness to us.

If we keep on waiting for retirement to be generous we might never get the opportunity. Midlife is a good time to start putting to good use what God has given us.

You've learned a few things about life ... Share it with the younger blokes

There are many positives about aging that far outweigh the saggy elbows, or slower running times. As you grow older, you often are further up the ladder in business, or politics, or in your chosen career and gain a degree of power and I don't mean power in a structural sense. As men grow older and wiser from experience they will grow in relational power or influence.

Our society is busy heading down the track of being stupid, youth-obsessed, and dismissive of the aged. But there is still a lot of capital left in respect for the older man. Older men's wise words carry more weight. The encouragement of an older person to a younger person can be powerful; a rebuke can cause great effect. We need to be deliberate and careful about how we use this power.

It's time to begin to be an elder in the tribe. I have lived away from home for about thirty years now since I was eighteen. Grafton is 600kms away from where I live. I ring Mum and Dad each week so I talk to my Dad regularly. As I look back on my life, as well as my dad there have been at least two other key men, one the same age as my dad and the other a little younger. These men have been there to help me through the stages of life, and through some hard times. Just talking with older men who have been through what I'm going through, and have some wisdom, is a great help. I'm now trying to do that with younger men as well, and I want to encourage you to do the same. The influence you could have on a younger man may be much greater than you imagine.

Conclusion
A life full of meaning

There is no doubt that midlife can be a challenging time full of change and letting go of some of the good things about being young. Just how we embrace these changes can make all the difference to what lies ahead.

If we get to this stage thinking that we are alone in the universe and that we are just left to do the best we can with the limited years we have, then I think it's no wonder that, like Solomon, many men see life as having lost its sheen, and that all things are ultimately meaningless. Glory days (if we ever had them) have well and truly passed us by.

But, with a word from beyond the sun from God; with God himself turning up in our midst, as wild an idea as that is, I reckon everything is turned on its head. To have the opportunity to follow Jesus—the one true King—into midlife and beyond, makes every bit of difference. It is both a simple and an immeasurably profound thing.

With this in mind, life becomes anything but meaningless. We actually live in a world that is charged with the electricity of eternity.

The climactic picture of the Bible comes in the book of Revelation, where the Apostle John has this great vision of the future, a vision of the judgment day and what happens beyond that. It's an awesome picture where evil is done away with finally and decisively, and then we get this sensational image of hope in the promised new creation:

Then I saw a new heaven and a new earth, for the first heaven and the first earth had passed away, and there was no longer any sea. I saw the Holy City, the New Jerusalem, coming down out of heaven from God, prepared as a bride beautifully dressed for her husband. And I heard a loud voice from the throne saying, "Now the dwelling of God is with men, and he will live with them. They will be his people, and God himself will be with them and be their God. He will wipe every tear from their eyes. There will be no more death or mourning or crying or pain, for the old order of things has passed away" (Revelation 21:1–4).

In light of all this, the mundane now becomes meaningful because of what lies behind it, a creator God who made us all, who has gone to great lengths to be in a relationship with us, and who stands behind his creation as the one in whom all our activities find their purpose. It now matters how I approach each day, as a day that has significance in eternity; as a day where it matters to God how I treat other people and how others treat me. There is profound significance in the job that I do and in the way that I do it. I can be assured, (or I suppose concerned) that the way I speak to my wife and kids matters. It matters how I relate to the people I work for and who work for me.

I reckon this perspective even has a bearing on things like the way I prepare a meal, or clean my house, or take care of my aging parents: because I now know I am operating within the realm of a revolutionary kingdom, that is of the future, but also is a present reality. When we take our cues from the God of the Bible, we can know that things like caring for the local environment, or being generous to friends, or working with dedication and efficiency is not a lost or futile effort or meaningless, but actually has even greater significance because the God who created the universe, also created us, and our community.

The flip side of all this is to ask ourselves 'Does it matter how much money I have or if I have the latest cars or houses? Does it matter if I get to the top of the corporate ladder? Does it matter that I am getting older and have lost my youth?'

What matters is how we treat God. Do we honour him, fear him and thank him and because of that do we treat other people the right way, being engaged with the world he has put us in? In response to God's generosity to us have we been generous; have we cared for others and have we cared for his creation? That's what matters. When we live in the light of eternity we can afford to live sacrificially, generously and selflessly because we know that this life is not all there is. We can face the rest of life as a great opportunity to get in tune with what God is doing in the world.

We still live in a world of frustration. We still live in some ways under the sun; we still feel the futility and the meaninglessness, but following Jesus allows us to avoid living in a value system that operates only under the sun. We don't get sucked in to living as if this is all there is. We are free to live in the light of eternity. To me that makes the pain and struggle of midlife pale into insignificance. It is my hope that you too will come to have that perspective and that along with other men who follow Jesus, we can get on with living lives of meaning and purpose; of hope, service and love.

Bibliography

Steve Biddulph, *Manhood—An Action Plan For Changing Men's Lives*, Finch Publishing, Sydney, 1994, 1995, 2002.

Robert Bly, *Iron John*, Addison–Wesley Publishing Company Incorporated, USA, 1990.

Bob Buford, *Halftime—Changing your game plan from success to significance*, Harper Collins/Zondervan, Grand Rapids, Michigan, 1994.

Gary D Chapman, *The Five Love Languages; How to express heartfelt commitment to your mate*, Northfield Publishing, 1992, 1995.

Paul Davies, *The Mind of God—The Science And The Search For Ultimate Meaning*, Penguin Books Ltd, London, England, 1992.

Alain de Botton, *Status Anxiety*, Pantheon Books, New York, 2004.

Tom L Eisenman, *Temptations Men Face, Straightforward Talk on Power, Money, Affairs, Perfectionism, Insensitivity*, Intervarsity Press, Downers Grove, Illinois, 1990.

John Eldredge, *Wild at Heart—discovering the secret of a man's soul*, Thomas Nelson Inc., Nashville, Tennessee, 2001.

Nigel Marsh, *Fat, Forty and Fired*, Bantam, Australia and New Zealand, 2005.

Appendix A

Men and midlife—exercise and the physical

By Dr John Best, B.Med, Dip Sports Medicine (London), FACSP, FFSEM, Sports Physician, Sports and Exercise Medicine

I. Introduction

Whether or not we are middle-aged, our inherent make up is a combination of how we function physically, mentally, and spiritually. All three are interconnected so that a healthy body will impact us in other important ways as well.

The ageing process affects all aspects of our makeup—in both positive and negative ways. Nevertheless, these changes may be managed in a very productive manner. This segment outlines the physiology of the ageing process, looking at the middle-age period as being a very exciting time of change, where good decisions may in fact lead to a healthier and more content life.

As mentioned in the main part of the book, over the last decade, American businessman and author Bob Buford has described middle age as being a 'half time' in the game of life. Many of you will appreciate this analysis of life as a game. It goes something like this... the **first half** of life may be considered as the period of age twenty to forty. It is a period of having a basic game plan, establishing foundations; once you kick off you start with great enthusiasm and a sense of adventure. You are trying to build and create things.

As life changes, you enter into a **half time** period. This may be between the ages of say forty to fifty-five. Often at this time many of your first half goals are achieved—getting on top of your mortgage, kids becoming less dependent, getting established in your work. This may be quite a liberating time but either way it is a time to reassess your game plan. At half time you need to reassess whether you need to make some changes to equip you to progress into the second half of your life.

The **second half** of living, therefore, is considered the period between the ages of 55 and 60 to the end of life on earth. During the second half, you're rechecking your game plan, you may have changed your strategies, but by and large you're keen to finish strongly. You may want to leave a mark on this world.

First half 20 – 40	Half time 40 – 55/60	Second Half > 55 / 60
Laying foundations	Review first half	Rechecking game plan
Establishing a game plan	Plan for second half	Changing strategies
Enthusiasm	Keen to finish strong	Adventure

Here we will focus very much on the midlife or half time phase.

ii. Physiology of ageing and middle age.

The physiology of ageing is an analysis of how the body works during the ageing process. At this point, you may be thinking, 'Here we go, we're in for some bad news', but let me tell you the bad news seems to start fairly early. Some researchers have found that even as early as the age of nine, in some children, the early process of cardio vascular disease (blocked arteries to the heart) may commence. As I'm getting a bit thin on top, I do remember one or two schoolmates who even during our last year of school, were starting to have a receding hairline—what we would often call the dreaded marching back, or the devon patch.

What we are interested in though is our ability to function. Can we keep moving well, can we think clearly, can we make good decisions, can we compete physically in certain areas that may interest us? Can we function sexually, can we get excited, can we enjoy the range of emotions that God designed us to feel? Let's take a look.

a. The body

'I'm getting old,' a patient said to me. He was distressed because he had suffered pain and swelling in his knee for two months. It was especially bad at night, or when going up and down stairs, and he was finding it difficult to bend down to do some general chores around the home. Even putting on his shoes and socks was becoming awkward. Oddly enough, the patient—Graham—was a forty-two year-old accountant, who had competed in many triathlons, had never had major injuries, was slim but had developed a knee problem, which he had not addressed initially. His knee problem was in fact quite simple, we managed to get it sorted out and he was back running almost three months later and has competed in triathlons since.

What amazed me about Graham was that he had started to think 'I'm getting old'. Men, from the outset I would suggest to you that if this is the way you are thinking, yes you are right, but you are also setting yourself up for a lot of disappointment. Ageing is a normal process that we shouldn't see as a negative. It's managing ageing that is really the key and the secret to unlocking some of the challenges.

i. Heart disease

This is the main killer in our age group. Many good studies since the 1950s have found that people who are inactive (sedentary) will have a 1.5 to 2-fold higher risk of major heart related events compared to people who are at least moderately active. We're talking here of heart attacks, heart failure and the development of blood pressure problems. A fascinating feature is that the introduction of physical activity significantly reduces this risk of heart disease, which may then lead to other improvements in health such as reducing obesity. Overall this will reduce other illness risks such as stroke and diabetes.

ii. Cancers

Do you know that being physically inactive causes around one fifth of all bowel cancers in the population? The common cancers in men include bowel cancer, prostate cancer, lung cancer and skin cancer. It is likely that you have had some experience with these either personally or through your relationships with others who have suffered cancer. This dreaded word provokes intense fear in many people. By and large, cancers are more common with the ageing process, but if detected early, are treatable.

A cancer specialist referred me a patient of his who had treatment for bowel cancer. Kevin was fifty-two years old, had done some boxing in the police force when he was younger, but really hadn't done much exercise from about the age of 30. A common story in Australia. Kevin had two operations for his bowel cancer, had some chemotherapy and took a long time to get back to a normal diet. He lost a huge amount of weight, felt frail and certainly felt very old.

The good news was that the cancer hadn't spread. Kevin was also in his half time period of life. He thought that it was time he 'pulled his finger out' and did something different. He proceeded to get involved with fundraising, running across Australia several times. You may know of Kevin as he had some press coverage, but the thing that was interesting was that once he started exercising, and enjoying physical training, he simply couldn't give it up. And as he said to me, 'Getting started in my head was the main problem. Once I got that right, I was fine and the body followed.' Men, if you think you're getting old, and accept that in a negative way, it will be very difficult for you to change your attitude. Accept ageing as a normal process and see what you can change to enjoy this time in your life.

iii. Diabetes

Up to ten per cent of adult Australians either have diabetes or a family history of diabetes. This may be insulin-dependent or non insulin-dependent. If untreated it can be a serious problem, with both eyesight and the nervous system being affected and the development of obesity.

Physical activity is a critical dimension in the management of diabetes. For both insulin and non-insulin dependent diabetics, the evidence is that the introduction of a more active lifestyle, dietary changes and weight loss, may in fact control the disease and reduce its severity. It may mean that an early (mild) diabetic could eliminate the disease.

iv. Musculoskeletal problems

The musculoskeletal system involves bones, joints and the soft tissues such as muscles and tendons. Both hard tissue (bone and joint) and the soft tissue (muscle and tendon) do change with ageing.

Most people connect ageing with arthritis. Arthritis is an inflammation of the joints and the most common type is osteoarthritis, which is the degeneration of joint surfaces. Many men consider it a death knell when they are told they have arthritis.

'My hip is gone', said Bill, aged forty-nine. Bill was a builder who played a lot of rugby league in his youth. There was a history of osteoarthritis in his family. His dad had had a knee replacement. Bill still enjoyed mucking around, playing some touch football, but he developed severe groin pain, which was keeping him up at night. On examination, he had a very stiff hip and x-rays revealed he had advanced osteoarthritis. Very clearly the arthritis has been there for quite some time. Despite our efforts to treat him without surgery, Bill ultimately needed a total hip replacement. Obviously, he was fairly young for this.

The good news with Bill is that he remained very motivated and didn't let this problem get him down. In his work as a builder, he was involved with more planning and management. He did some work on the tools. Interestingly, with regard to sport and exercise, he started getting involved with swimming and kayaking. Bill started a small swim squad at his local surf club in one of Australia's coastal towns.

Degenerative change in joints may be prevented with addressing injuries well, avoiding obesity, maintaining good strength in surrounding muscles and maintaining good alignment and footwear, particularly if you spend a lot of time standing or walking. The other non-operative strategies such as the use of various supplements (e.g. glucosamine / chondroitin) are useful but are beyond the scope of this book.

Muscle and tendon dysfunction is a little more interesting. In the early twenties, around the age of twenty to twenty-five, the release of growth hormone and the male sex hormone, testosterone, reduces. Many men who have regularly done weights notice that it is more difficult for them to maintain muscle mass and if they stop training for a few weeks they lose their muscle fairly quickly.

The good news is that there are significant training benefits to be gained with resistance (strength) exercises, which are really worth doing. This has many protective effects, such as giving a greater sense of wellbeing. It also protects you from tendon problems. Tendons are the extension of muscles. A muscle forms a tendon, which joins into a bone. For example, the calf muscle forms the achilles in the lower part of the leg, which anchors onto the heel bone. Tendons are like pieces of rope. There is some evidence now that tendons do wear down like a joint may wear down. Once again, you can protect this by avoiding obesity, maintaining strength and having good alignment and good footwear.

A summary of the physiology of ageing on the body

The middle-age period of life is where the more acute ageing changes may be identified. The development of blood pressure problems, diabetes, cholesterol, heart disease or arthritic change may appear at this time. It is absolutely critical that all men have a good relationship with their local General Practitioner, who they can come to, to have medical problems addressed promptly. Also, a sports physician may offer a more detailed assessment and exercise advice.

There is also good evidence that a once-per-year check up (medical screening) may identify risk factors to prevent further problems. This may be a simple physical examination, which may include a rectal examination, blood test and occasionally other tests, such as stress tests.

The physiological changes with ageing have been shown to affect people's attitude to their health. If you are someone who is disappointed about getting older and have resigned yourself to the fact that it's all down hill from here, well you've basically given in to your circumstances, and it is likely you will have trouble digging yourself out of the hole you are in. Most disappointingly, you may be missing out on great opportunities to turn things around, particularly if your problems are controllable or reversible. Very often the mind is affected in the aging process, and this needs to be taken into consideration.

b. The physiology of ageing on the mind

This section will look at cognitive function (the ability to think, concentrate and process information) and mental illness.

i. Cognitive function

The middle-age period may be the time when dementia starts to present itself. Dementia is a degenerative disorder of brain tissue. Its most common form is Alzheimer's disease, which is more commonly seen in men and women over the age of seventy years. There are other aggressive forms, which do present themselves early. Lapses in memory, particularly short-term memory, may be one of the presenting features. In addition, behavioural changes such as periods of depression or anger may also develop. Friends, family and others, more than the individual, often notice these.

Men, it is very important that if you have any concerns in this area, you have them addressed. There are advanced preventative measures these days, which may reduce the rate of any deterioration, but more importantly the diagnosis needs to be made. There are many tests of mental function, which are commonly known as neuro-psychometric tests (similar to the types of tests that are used to assess concussion in a footballer). Many drugs will worsen the condition. They include excessive use of alcohol, the use of marijuana or other illegal drugs (e.g. ecstasy, ice). I'm surprised as to how many men in their middle-age use social and recreational drugs, which are illegal. This may be the culture of some work environments, or social networks or it may be that life becomes too much for some men who then look for an escape. Of serious concern is the potential damage to the brain and other organs, which we just can't afford to place at risk.

ii. Mental illness

There is a continued stigma regarding mental illness in the community. In the middle-age group, these are commonly the 'affective disorders' and typically these are anxiety and depression. Research tells us that ten to thirty per cent of Australian men will suffer these problems at some point. Stress may be considered as a time of hardship or adversity where external pressure is exerted on the individual. Frankly, this is a part of life. You'll have your ups and downs and using a sporting analogy, this would be consistent with the game of life. The key really is ensuring that you are in a position to manage stress when it occurs and, at the same time, not allowing constant stress to have a negative effect.

Quite apart from normal stress though, individuals may have a separate medical problem, where they suffer with depression or anxiety. As mentioned, these affective disorders do impact on an individual's mood. It may also impact the body's function, leading to sleep difficulties, appetite change, altered sexual function, periods of anger, periods of crying which may all be associated factors. If there is stress, which is occurring at the same time, it may be difficult to differentiate whether or not someone's initial symptoms are from stress or if they are independent to the development of other problems such as depression and anxiety. Either way, men, this is where we can help each other and also help ourselves. Identifying behavioural changes, particularly if it's connected to disturbed sleep is very important. A diagnosis should be made as treatment is available and is very different for different conditions.

Certainly some of the challenges of middle-age can contribute to the development of depression. This may be a significant barrier to men making lifestyle changes. You may know that exercise is good for you, you may know how to do it, you may know that doing some exercise with your wife or children or mates is a good thing, but actually getting up and doing it may seem difficult. It is my own personal belief that this de-motivation contributes to a general feeling of tiredness and fatigue that many middle-age men experience.

Very importantly, men need to be able to talk about depression and not battle it out alone. Getting the right help can help avoid untold misery, not only for the sufferer, but for his family and friends as well.

c. Spiritual matters

The very successful rugby league coach, Wayne Bennett, has said, 'If a footballer is not happy off the field, he won't be at his best on the field'. I heard him speak about this at a conference when he went on to talk about the importance of having your off field matters, home life, personal relationships and personal desires in order, so that you can function well physically. Spiritual matters come with different connotations but really we're addressing the issues which affect our deepest personal needs, our soul, our insides, and the area that may possibly drive every other part of our lives.

I strongly endorse the message of this book in helping men in mid-life and beyond, not only to get the physical part right, but crucially, the spiritual as well.

Websites offering free information on health and fitness are:

Dr John Best at Orthosports: www.orthosports.com.au

or

The Australasian College of Sports Physicians: www.acsp.org.au

or

Sports Medicine Australia: www.sma.org.au

Appendix B

Men & midlife— middle-aged men and sex

By Dr Amelia Haines – MBBS (Syd), Dip. Sexual Health Counselling, Sexual Health Practitioner

Introduction

I feel kind of alien as I think about writing a chapter on sex in a book for men, and aging men at that. That being said, I like men, I like aging men and I like talking about, writing about, reading about and having sex.

So let me start by encouraging you mature and maturing males by destroying the myth that a man's 'sexual peak' is in his late teens. In fact, there is a very good argument that a man's 'sexual prime' only begins in his late thirties and continues to his life's end. Maybe the teenage peak myth refers to something we might call a 'genital peak'. When a boy goes through puberty and is fully mature, he is able to get an erection, ejaculate and get an erection and ejaculate again quickly (the time period between ejaculation and being able to get another erection is called the refractory period). But even at seventeen, this refractory period extends if he masturbates or copulates a number of times (let's face it, we're not taking about making love here!).

Unfortunately, people have actually studied such behaviour in laboratories. As you age, your refractory period also increases. At seventy or eighty, it might even be a week in length. So changes you may have noticed in yourself in this area are entirely consistent with growing up. But there is an up side: men in their sexual prime start to have the potential to be better lovers and require better quality sexual environments for a really good time.

The above facts could either delight or distress your wife or partner, depending on the state of your relationship, your health and your wellbeing. But let's just talk about you for a while longer.

Perhaps you are very interested in the conditions for a good sexual experience, or maybe you've never had to think much about it and have functioned pretty much automatically. Either way, as you get older, as a sexual experience goes badly, or as you lose your job, or your relationship changes in some way, your sexual system can become disrupted. At this point, men need to readjust their sexual patterns.

Some changes men may experience as they get older are:

1. You need to feel connected and close to your wife or partner. This is usually seen as a 'woman's requirement' but a lot of men need it too. To spell this out: when you're grumpy with her, you don't enjoy sex, or even still want it. You need the relationship to be going well in order to want and enjoy sex.

2. You release yourself from anxiety about sexual performance. You either feel good about your ability to please your wife or partner, or you start to believe that if things don't progress in a 'Hollywood sex' way it will still be fine with her.

3. You start to feel more secure about your partner or wife's attitude to engaging in sexual behaviour, her response to your stimulation and overtures, and her stimulation of you.

4. You tend to be fairly well, not so anxious about work or study, not preoccupied or under the influence of drugs and /or alcohol to the extent you may have been during your misspent youth. (An A+ for anyone who doesn't understand this point at all.)

5. You feel more positive and less anxious before sex is even initiated—you're interested, you know she is, and you think you'll have fun.

6. You start to need increased interest and adequate tactile stimulation to perform sexually. Remember, morning erections do not necessarily indicate sexual interest! Also, as many will have discovered now, sometimes you are interested but the erection is just not there.

The maturing penis

As a man ages several changes occur in the physiology and anatomy of the penis. To begin with, the angle of erection is less acute. It doesn't point to the heavens anymore and gradually points more and more straight out from the body. An important reason for this is arterial health. The penis is like a window to the heart—literally. The changes of *arteriosclerosis* (hardening of the arteries) and *atherosclerosis* (getting cholesterol/fatty plaques on your arteries) don't just occur in the heart of a male, but in penile arteries to a very similar degree. This may be a more than usually motivating reason for you to give up smoking, reduce fatty foods and alcohol and go to your general practitioner to check your blood pressure and cholesterol. Just like a regular walk or other form of exercise, the penis also needs exercise. The old line 'use it or lose it' is truer than you thought. A nice regular erection feeds oxygen-rich blood to the penis keeping the tissues healthier. The erect penis also gets less firm with age, slower to fill with blood and become erect, and faster to empty (that is, to lose erection post-ejaculation). But the most important fact to remember about the maturing penis is that it still feels pleasure; undaunted by the passing years it retains the capacity to bring pleasure to its owner.

Impotence and premature ejaculation

I often say to my patients, 'only nice men get these difficulties', which is very true in several ways. Premature ejaculation only matters if you want couple pleasure to last longer and there are significant numbers of men who don't care too much about their partners responsiveness and enjoyment! And almost 100% of men will experience impotence at some time in their lives. When you are younger it is because you may be thinking too much, or caring about your ability to please your partner too much—things that increase anxiety lead to a decrease in 'performance'.

Impotence refers to loss of the ability to get and sustain an erection with enough rigidity to enable penetration. As men age, impotence needs to be analysed by a doctor for physical causes. Having said this, impotence often becomes a vicious cycle because once experienced, anxiety is naturally increased during subsequent sexual encounters, so it can become self-perpetuating even if physical causes are corrected. Drugs like Viagra/Levitra/Cialis are very useful for correcting confidence problems and in most instances will only need to be used briefly.

Premature ejaculation has a shifting medical definition (how many thrusts is too few?) but can be thought of as climaxing 'too soon'. Some men despair because they only last twenty minutes in intercourse and their partner is still not satisfied. Some women would find twenty minutes an insult! It is really useful to remember that sexual arousal is made up of physical stimulation *and* psychological stimulation. When novelty is involved, sexual arousal occurs more quickly, even with the same level of physical stimulation. Hence couples who have the same rapid ejaculation problems opt for the minimal physical stimulation (until the last minute) because there is so much background psychological stimulation (and/or anxiety). This is not a stupid idea and many solid relationships are built around this. At the same time, as you age your penis requires more direct physical stimulation to become erect, and many wives may need to change the habits of a lifetime and become more involved in penile stimulation. No one has a fail-safe 'cure' for premature ejaculation. There are many things that can help, most of which require some motivation to employ. Normally it just needs the couple involved to make adjustments to their habits. There are also some antidepressants that work very well because one of their side effects is orgasmic 'retardation'. Drugs advertised on radio and TV must be treated as unhelpful and avoided. Remember, only nice, intelligent, thoughtful men have these sexual hiccups—and we women in the real world, prefer you every time.

Vasectomy

This is a simple procedure to stop sperm being ejaculated in the seminal fluid and thereby giving permanent birth control. Obviously, it is not an ethical option for some people, but for those for whom birth control is acceptable it is increasingly popular. A lot of women feel well-treated because their husbands take responsibility for birth control and free them from medication or another gynaecological procedure. Men often worry there will be a decrease in sexual interest or reduced performance; let me put those anxious minds to rest. Desire is in no way related to the *vas deferens* being in one piece, there is minimal decrease in ejaculation volume and no performance ramifications. It's a very safe procedure, and while all surgery has risks—there are not as many as in childbirth.

Please be brave and have your prostate examined. It's not that bad... really. Why not have it examined every year on your birthday so you don't forget? Or on an annual holiday so you don't have to see that particular doctor again? You think I jest? These are techniques used by women for the equally irritating need for yearly pap smears.

Examine your testicles or train someone you know and love to do it for you. The very worst thing you can do to your family is to die from a treatable disease. We love you.

Endnotes

1. P J O'Rourke, *All the trouble in the world*, Atlantic Monthly Press, New York, 1994, page 2.
2. *CIA's World Fact Book 2006*—quoted in the Good Weekend—SMH October 28, 2006.
3. Rodney Stark, *The Rise of Christianity*, Harper Collins, USA, 1997, page 155. Technically this is correct although misleading. If you made it to 4 or 5 years old the chances are you would live well into what we would consider adulthood. The figures are skewed by the high infant mortality rates. Over the past 20 years life expectancy has improved by 6.1 years for males and 4.5 years for females. A boy born in 2003—2005 can expect to live 78.5 years while a girl can expect to live 83.3 years.
4. Clive Hamilton and Richard Denniss, *Affluenza*, Allen & Unwin, Australia, 2005, page 118.
5. Having presided over a successful 1999 summit on drugs the Premier, who lost a brother to heroin, tried to explain drug ruination thus: 'Life is an inherently disappointing experience for most human beings.' He acknowledged drug users' propensity 'to compensate for the mediocrity of existence'. David Humphries, *Timing ripe for graceful exit*, Sydney Morning Herald, July 28, 2005.
6. The movie *Groundhog Day* is the story of Phil Connors (Bill Murray) who is sent to cover the Groundhog Day Festival in Punxsutawney, Pennsylvania on February 2nd—obviously in the middle of winter in the U.S. The movie shows Bill Murray caught in some kind of time warp, which means every morning he wakes up it is February 2nd and he is stuck in Punxsutawney, Pennsylvania, and there is nothing he can do to get out of the town. He is sentenced to live this same day in the same place again and again and again. (It is an excellent movie I recommend if you haven't already seen it.)

7. Biddulph, *Manhood*, page 1.

8. Biddulph, *Manhood*, page 7.

9. Biddulph, *Manhood*, page 15.

10. Biddulph, *Manhood*, page 198

11. Robert Bly, *Iron John*, Addison and Wesley, USA, 1990, page 81.

12. Ed Sissman, quoted in Eldridge, *Wild at heart*, page 43.

13. Quoted in Norman L Geisler and Paul K Hoffman (Eds) *Why I am a Christian*, Baker Books, Grand Rapids, Michigan, page 271.

14. Nigel Marsh, *Fat, Forty and Fired*, Random House Australia, page 132.

15. Marsh, page 133.

16. SKIN—Spend Kids Inheritance Now

17. Ecclesiastes 2:1–11

> 1 The words of the Teacher, son of David, king in Jerusalem:
>
> 2 "Meaningless! Meaningless!"
>
> says the Teacher.
>
> "Utterly meaningless!
>
> Everything is meaningless."
>
> 3 What does man gain from all his labor
>
> at which he toils under the sun?
>
> 4 Generations come and generations go,
>
> but the earth remains forever.
>
> 5 The sun rises and the sun sets,
>
> and hurries back to where it rises.
>
> 6 The wind blows to the south
>
> and turns to the north;
>
> round and round it goes,
>
> ever returning on its course.
>
> 7 All streams flow into the sea,
>
> yet the sea is never full.
>
> To the place the streams come from,
>
> there they return again.

8 All things are wearisome,

> more than one can say.

> The eye never has enough of seeing,

> nor the ear its fill of hearing.

9 What has been will be again,

> what has been done will be done again;

> there is nothing new under the sun.

10 Is there anything of which one can say,

> "Look! This is something new"?

> It was here already, long ago;

> it was here before our time.

11 There is no remembrance of men of old,

> and even those who are yet to come

> will not be remembered

> by those who follow.

18. Ravi Zacharias, in Norman L Geisler and Paul K Hoffman (eds) *Why I am a Christian—leading thinkers explain why they believe*, Baker Books, Grand Rapids, Michigan, 2001, page 271.

19. Ecclesiastes 2:1–11

Pleasures Are Meaningless

1 I thought in my heart, "Come now, I will test you with pleasure to find out what is good." But that also proved to be meaningless. 2 "Laughter," I said, "is foolish. And what does pleasure accomplish?" 3 I tried cheering myself with wine, and embracing folly—my mind still guiding me with wisdom. I wanted to see what was worthwhile for men to do under heaven during the few days of their lives. 4 I undertook great projects: I built houses for myself and planted vineyards. 5 I made gardens and parks and planted all kinds of fruit trees in them. 6 I made reservoirs to water groves of flourishing trees. 7 I bought male and female slaves and had other slaves who were born in my house. I also owned more herds and flocks than anyone in Jerusalem before me. 8 I amassed silver and gold for myself, and the treasure of kings and provinces. I acquired men

and women singers, and a harem as well—the delights of the heart of man. 9 I became greater by far than anyone in Jerusalem before me. In all this my wisdom stayed with me. 10 I denied myself nothing my eyes desired; I refused my heart no pleasure. My heart took delight in all my work, and this was the reward for all my labor. 11 Yet when I surveyed all that my hands had done and what I had toiled to achieve, everything was meaningless, a chasing after the wind; nothing was gained under the sun.

20. It is interesting to see that Bill Gates has given away approximately half his wealth to the Gates Foundation to combat diseases around the world. Good for him!

21. The Good Weekend, *Sydney Morning Herald*, April 7, 2007.

22. Ecclesiates 2:17–23

Toil Is Meaningless

17 So I hated life, because the work that is done under the sun was grievous to me. All of it is meaningless, a chasing after the wind. 18 I hated all the things I had toiled for under the sun, because I must leave them to the one who comes after me. 19 And who knows whether he will be a wise man or a fool? Yet he will have control over all the work into which I have poured my effort and skill under the sun. This too is meaningless. 20 So my heart began to despair over all my toilsome labor under the sun. 21 For a man may do his work with wisdom, knowledge and skill, and then he must leave all he owns to someone who has not worked for it. This too is meaningless and a great misfortune. 22 What does a man get for all the toil and anxious striving with which he labors under the sun? 23 All his days his work is pain and grief; even at night his mind does not rest. This too is meaningless.

23. Ecclesiastes 5:10–15

> 10 Whoever loves money never has money enough;
>
> whoever loves wealth is never satisfied with his income.
>
> This too is meaningless.
>
> 11 As goods increase,
>
> so do those who consume them.
>
> And what benefit are they to the owner
>
> except to feast his eyes on them?
>
> 12 The sleep of a laborer is sweet,
>
> whether he eats little or much,
>
> but the abundance of a rich man
>
> permits him no sleep.
>
> 13 I have seen a grievous evil under the sun:
>
> wealth hoarded to the harm of its owner,
>
> 14 or wealth lost through some misfortune,
>
> so that when he has a son
>
> there is nothing left for him.
>
> 15 Naked a man comes from his mother's womb,
>
> and as he comes, so he departs.
>
> He takes nothing from his labor
>
> that he can carry in his hand.

24. Tom Eisenman in his book *Temptations Men Face* analyses twelve steps that lead to adultery (sometimes called an affair). The twelve may be summarised quickly as:

   1. The condition of emotional readiness—something is occurring in a man's life that has him leaning away from his marriage.

   2. The second stage in the affair process is growing awareness of a particular person in our web of relationships.

   3. Innocent meeting—that's during the time of heightened awareness of the other women there can be truly innocent chance meetings, often legitimate chance business contacts that can potentially build the relationship.

   4. Intentional meetings—meetings occur frequently which appear to be by chance when in reality one person has acted in such a way as to increase the likelihood of meeting.

5. Public lingering—the man and the women now spend time together while in group settings. They tend to shut others out by turning away from the group and avoiding eye contact with others.

6. Private lingering—soon the man and the women find that they are still together long after others have left, there is now a growing excitement in being together alone.

7. Purposeful isolating—now the man and women begin to plan times alone for 'legitimate' purposes.

8. Pleasurable isolating—now the man and women are planning times alone with each other for the sheer enjoyment and fun of being together. The relationship takes on a youthful euphoria.

9. Affectionate embracing—secret longings for each other become intense—there is an embracing without letting go.

10. Passionate embracing—affectionate touching and embracing lead to passionate interchanges, when alcohol is involved the couple moves quickly through these stages.

11. Capitulation—the couple gives into sexual intercourse, denial is eliminated at this stage, there is no way they can deny the reality of what has occurred between them.

12. Acceptance—here the man and the woman admit to themselves and to each other that they are truly having an affair.

25. One movie where Hollywood did get it right about the consequences of adultery was *Fatal Attraction* starring Michael Douglas and Glenn Close. If you haven't seen it and you are considering adultery watch it, it will scare the pants "on" you.

26. Simon Castles, 'In the grip of guilty pleasure', *The Sunday Age*, October 8, 2006.

27. Jan LaRue, 'Obscenity and the First Amendment.' Summit on Pornography. Rayburn House Office Building. Room 2322. May 19, 2005.

28. Family Safe Media, December 15, 2005.

29. Family Safe Media, January 10, 2006.

30. *Christianity Today*, Leadership survey, December 2001.

31. Family Safe Media, December 15, 2005.

32. Covenant eyes—web site
http://www.covenanteyes.com/help_and_support/article/?a=151

33. Naomi Wolf, 'The Porn Myth', *New York Magazine*,
http://nymag.com/nymetro/news/trends/n_9437/ accessed 24/4/07.

34. Cornelius Plantinger, Jr. *Not the way it's supposed to be—a breviary of sin*, Eerdmans Publishing Company, Grand Rapids, Michigan, 1995, page 2.

35. When the Apostle Paul writes about the creation being subjected to frustration (in Greek) the word he uses has the same meaning as the word 'meaningless', (meaninglessness in Hebrew) in Ecclesiastes.

36. Copernicus is credited with the discovery that the earth was not the centre of the universe and that the earth revolved around the sun.

37. Bertrand Russell quoted in
http://www.apologetics.fsnet.co.uk/eternity.htm viewed June 1, 2007.

38. Paul Davies *The Mind of God—Science and the search for ultimate meaning*, Penguin Books Ltd, 27 Wrights Lane, London, England, 1992, page 232.

39. Ravi Zacharias, in Norman L Geisler and Paul K Hoffman (eds) *Why I am a Christian—Leading thinkers explain why they believe*, Baker Books, Grand Rapids, Michigan, 2001 page 267.

40. C S Lewis, *Mere Christianity*, Fount—an imprint of Harper Collins Publishers, London, UK, 1997, page 187.

41. 1 Corinthians 15:32.

42. Being at the bottom of the pecking order at the Roosters could be a problem.

43. 'Son of Man' is another title Jesus used for himself.

44. John Stott, *Why I am a Christian*, Intervarsity Press, United Kingdom, 2003, page 94.

45. Matthew, Mark, Luke or John in the New Testament.

46. Biddhulph, page 72.